"Too often, there is a huge gap between the comprehensive services provided to children with ASD in school and the options available when they become adults. THE AUTISM TRANSITION GUIDE helps families, service providers, and adults with ASD to build bridges across that gap to a satisfying adulthood. A valuable guide for everyone involved in the transition process."

—Diana M. Katovitch, MS, Special Education Teacher
author of THE POWER TO SPRING UP: POSTSECONDARY EDUCATION OPPORTUNITIES
FOR STUDENTS WITH SIGNIFICANT DISABILITIES

The Autism Transition Guide

TOPICS IN AUTISM

The Autism Transition Guide

PLANNING THE JOURNEY FROM SCHOOL TO ADULT LIFE

**Carolyn Thorwarth Bruey, Psy.D.
& Mary Beth Urban, M.Ed.**

Sandra L. Harris, Ph.D., series editor

Woodbine House ◆ 2009

All rights reserved. Published in the United States of America by Woodbine House, Inc.,
6510 Bells Mill Road, Bethesda, MD 20817. 800-843-7323. www.woodbinehouse.com

Library of Congress Cataloging-in-Publication Data

Bruey, Carolyn Thorwarth.
  The autism transition guide : planning the journey from school to adult life / Carolyn
Thorwarth Bruey and Mary Beth Urban. -- 1st ed.
      p. cm. -- (Topics in autism)
  Includes bibliographical references and index.
  ISBN 978-1-890627-81-2
  1. Autistic children--Education. I. Urban, Mary Beth. II. Title.
  LC4717.B78 2009
  371.94--dc22
                                                                                    2009015539

Manufactured in the United States of America

First Edition

10   9   8   7   6   5   4   3   2   1

To my children, Will and Frances,
who are launching into adulthood,
as well as my loving husband, Paul,
who is sharing the ride with me.
~Carolyn T. Bruey

To my husband, Mike, and family
who supported me in this endeavor,
and to my father, Frank, whose work ethic
and value system remains instilled in me.
~Mary Beth Urban

Table of Contents

Introduction

Parenting or working with adolescents as they make the transition into adulthood is not for the faint of heart. When the adolescent has an autism spectrum disorder, going through this transition can seem downright daunting. Not only are parents and professionals faced with the typical challenges of adolescence such as hormonal changes and increased urges for independence, but they also have the intimidating task of making serious and potentially life-altering decisions about the individual's future path as he or she enters adulthood.

This book is meant to be a resource for parents and professionals who are faced with such an endeavor. We will provide guidance on making the transition from adolescence to adulthood as smooth and stress-free an experience as possible for everyone involved, including the individual with an autism spectrum disorder (ASD). Focusing on issues that often crop up when the young person is between the ages of fourteen through the early twenties, we will offer information that should help parents and professionals better understand what is involved and to create viable strategies which can facilitate a smooth "launching" into adulthood.

What Are Autism Spectrum Disorders?

Since this book focuses on adolescence and early adulthood, you are most likely already more than knowledgeable regarding autism spectrum disorders. However, let's briefly review some of the more salient characteristics of individuals with ASDs. First, the primary areas of concern with individuals with ASDs are: 1) qualitative impairments in social skills, 2) qualitative impairments in communication, and 3) the presence of ritualistic and repetitive activities or interests. However, the way in which any given person with this diagnosis manifests the "triad of symptoms" varies widely, and you will never meet two individuals with an ASD who are exactly alike.

It is also important to note that there are five types of autism spectrum disorders: 1) Autistic Disorder, 2) Asperger's Disorder, 3) Rett's Disorder, 4) Childhood Disintegrative Disorder, and 5) Pervasive Developmental Disorder-Not Otherwise Specified (PDD-NOS). Providing specific information about each of these disorders is beyond the scope of this book. We recommend you refer to our list of resources at the end of the book if you are interested in gaining greater insight regarding diagnostic criteria, instructional strategies, or other resource information for a specific disorder. Due to the relatively low incidence of Rett's Disorder and Childhood Disintegrative Disorder, the present book will focus only on interventions and issues that are relevant to Autism, Asperger's Disorder, and Pervasive Developmental Disorder-Not Otherwise Specified.

What Will You Learn from Reading This Book?

This book reviews a wide variety of topics and strategies. First, in Chapter One we provide an overview of the various living and work options that you may consider when planning for individuals with an ASD as they reach adulthood. In Chapter Two, we provide a legal framework that you can use when developing a transition plan. A review of federal mandates and educational requirements will give you a basis upon which to build a legally sound roadmap. It is important for parents and professionals to understand how legislation such as No Child Left Behind (NCLB) affects the overall transition process. We also provide techniques that can be used to choose educational goals that best address the strengths, passions, and needs of a given individual with an ASD.

Chapter Three addresses the need for cooperative and supportive teamwork amongst all involved parties when a young person with ASD is transitioning from high school to the community. Parents, community agencies, job trainers, school personnel, and the individual with an ASD need to work together seamlessly with clear, shared goals. Everyone's responsibilities and follow-up roles in regards to the student's transition need to be spelled out and monitored. As you will see, at times it is effective for the transition team to periodically break out into focus groups so that everyone involved can use his or her own area of expertise. We also outline how to make sure that everyone stays committed and focused during the transition process.

We have broken down the transition process from early adolescence to graduation from high school into three phases: early, middle, and approaching graduation. As reviewed in Chapter Four, during each phase it is important to address and update employment opportunities, possible living arrangements, self-help/daily living skills, and community involvement and networking issues that may need to be considered and revisited to facilitate a successful transition. We also suggest ways to monitor progress as the student nears graduation and then enters the workforce in order to assure that everyone is still on the same track and that all needed adjustments have been made. We also point out supports that can be set up throughout this process to prepare the student with an ASD, his or her parents, and the community as the transition takes place.

It is often difficult to gauge just how involved the individual with an ASD should be during the transition from school to adulthood. Of course, this depends upon each individual's cognitive and emotional status and therefore there is no one right answer. As we all know, the autism spectrum is a wide one and therefore decisions regarding when and how to involve a particular student with an ASD must be individualized. Chapter Five provides guidelines regarding how to take advantage of each student's strengths in order to assure that he or she has the opportunity to participate in the transition process as fully as possible.

Once a young adult with an autism spectrum disorder has graduated from high school, it is essential to create monitoring systems and supports in order to assure that he or she continues to flourish. Chapter Six, "Beyond School," therefore reviews strategies for helping the individual succeed as he or she learns to adapt to new expectations of adulthood. In Chapter Seven we provide a tool for documenting the transition process, as well as case studies that describe how the strategies reviewed in this book have been applied to four students transitioning from school to adulthood. This will hopefully help parents and professionals "put it all together." Finally, Chapter Eight offers our concluding comments, including suggestions for helping everyone involved to respond effectively to the emotional roller coaster inherent to transition.

General Themes Regarding Transitioning from School to Adulthood

Throughout this book, you will encounter many ideas and recommendations. Let's start by outlining some of the principal themes we would like you to remember:

Individualize, individualize, individualize: Young people with an ASD can vary greatly in terms of their abilities, ranging from those with limited or no speech who may require twenty-four hour supervision, to those who will be able to attend college or obtain competitive employment. Therefore, each transition plan needs to be highly individualized for each unique student. For example, an integral part of the transition process is to choose goals for the student's Individualized Education Program (IEP) that are truly individualized and will assure that the student has the necessary skills prior to graduating from high school.

Start ASAP: When should you start planning for transition? Our overall message is, "you can never begin too early." Unfortunately, many parents and professionals wait until the student is nearing graduation before they truly focus on transition. However, it can be difficult to develop the necessary networking framework, let alone teach the required skills to the student, if you begin the process so close to graduation. Most educational guidelines mandate that transition should begin to be addressed when the student is fourteen years to sixteen years of age. However, it is often helpful to think about transition when the student is even younger. Parents and professionals need to start carving out a realistic image of the student with ASD as an adult and begin to set up the educational and community scaffolding in order to obtain that image with plenty of time to see the plan to fruition.

Recognize that transition is a difficult time for everyone: All parents find transition to be a complicated process as their children approach young adulthood. Allowing increased independence while continuing to provide necessary support is a difficult balance to achieve, even for parents of typically developing offspring. It can also be a stressful and confusing time for individuals with ASD due to the increased pressure and the multitude of changes involved. Parents whose children have an ASD often feel ambivalence, fear, and anxiety. In fact, many parents note that their child's twenty-first birthday is an especially traumatic experience because the day is often clouded by the realization that the child's "launching" into adulthood will look significantly different compared to that of typically developing twenty-one-year-olds.

Emotions during transition can also be quite positive as parents and professionals watch the individual with an ASD excel in a vocation that matches his or her abilities and interests. Parents in particular usually feel pride and perhaps some degree of relief when their adult child with an ASD gains employment or moves out of the family home. Of special note, young adults with an ASD often feel proud of *themselves* as they gain increased independence. Remember, the natural evolution of a family is from the parent(s) alone, to the parent(s) with children, followed by a return to the parent(s) alone. Although adults with ASDs may need more support than typical young adults, they nonetheless have the right to live as independent a life as possible. In Chapter Eight, we provide suggestions regarding how you can respond to the emotional issues in "letting go."

Educate yourself about research and supports for transition: Unfortunately, most research literature and funding seem to be focused on the earlier years of a child with an ASD (e.g., early intervention programs). The transition from school to adulthood has been relatively ignored and therefore parents and professionals are often left to their own instincts when going through this process. Nonetheless, we will attempt to provide you with the most current, up-to-date guidelines and strategies so that you can hopefully feel more capable of responding successfully.

Keep in mind the "Triad of Symptoms" when planning for transition: It is often advantageous to keep in mind the three core domains of an autism spectrum disorder—qualitative impairments in social skills, qualitative impairments in communication, and the presence of ritualistic/repetitive interests or actions—during transition. For example, choosing IEP goals related to improving these core deficits, while incorporating the individual's passions, will help the student acquire the necessary skills prior to graduating from high school.

Understand the difference between "giving up" and having realistic goals: Planning for the student's future when graduation from high school is still seven or eight years down the road can be a difficult task. Parents and professionals often feel concerned about "giving up" on academically-oriented goals if the decision is made to focus primarily upon prevocational or vocational skills. Of course, for the more cognitively adept student with an ASD, it often makes sense to continue teaching traditional academics from the general education curriculum. However, for most individuals with ASDs, understanding the concepts underlying a mathematical problem is less important than learning how to use a calculator. After all, when was the last time you balanced your checkbook by hand? Also, forcing a student to study academic subjects that are too difficult often leads to an increase in challenging behaviors due to the student's frustration and inability to perform. Therefore, parents and professionals alike need to weigh the advantages and disadvantages of each and every IEP goal in order to make sure that the individual has functional skills that will serve him or her well upon entering adulthood.

In Sum

We recognize that helping young people with autism spectrum disorders make the transition from school to work and community life involves an overwhelming number of steps and potential obstacles that make it seem intimidating to everyone involved. We hope that this book will provide hands-on strategies and insights that will prove helpful to you as you experience this important journey.

1 | Where Are We Headed?

"If you don't know where you are going, you will probably end up somewhere else."

—Lawrence J. Peter

One of the first steps to take when helping a student with an autism spectrum disorder make the transition into adulthood is to gain a clear vision of where you want to be when the process is complete. If you are unaware of the multitude of available options, it is virtually impossible to generate this vision. This chapter seeks to fill in any gaps in your knowledge by providing an overall framework of the possibilities for both employment and living arrangements. Once you know what options exist, you will be better equipped to develop a realistic, individualized transition plan.

The best way to develop comprehensive transition plans for students with autism spectrum disorders is to begin with the end and work backwards. In the United States, this is most often accomplished by writing a "Statement of Transition Services" in the student's Individualized Education Program (IEP). This statement is intended to be a clear plan for what your child will know and be able to do after high school. It is a step-by-step guide to instruction so that the student will be prepared for life when he graduates from (or ages out of) high school. All members who are involved in planning for transition, including parents, school staff, and the student himself, must develop a clear vision of the student's life as an adult. This vision must include:

- What the child will do immediately after completing high school—postsecondary education, competitive or supported employment, or a structured day program;
- Where he will live after graduation and how he will get help with activities of daily living;
- An idea of how the individual will participate in the community after he leaves school.

When your child is just entering his teens, it can be difficult to think about what may not occur for six to ten years. But when you have a child with an autism spectrum disorder, it is imperative to plan ahead so that you are not caught off guard. In fact, there are many issues to consider and plan for as early as possible in the student's educational career. Until age 21, he may be entitled to specially designed instruction as a result of his disability. But, once he graduates, the entitlements to education stop and supports are limited. Families must pay for postsecondary education and the supports their child may need to benefit from training. The Statement of Transition Services will help your family to determine exactly what services your child could benefit from before he leaves high school and help you determine how to get it.

Transition planning will also give you and your family a better understanding of the skills that your child needs to acquire in order to meet his own goals as well as your goals for him. The well-designed plan will work backwards from your family's vision to the present time and systematically lay out the instruction and supports that are needed to attain that goal.

It is vital to set high expectations for your child, the educational team, and yourselves. At the same time, it is even more important to remain open-minded and to analyze the data and progress that your child is making each year so that the vision can be adjusted as necessary. Everyone is entitled to a dream. Yet, for a child with ASD, there needs to be some flexibility in realizing that dream, based on the practical realities and successes along the way.

Options to Consider for Postsecondary Activities

As with typically developing ("neurotypical") students, there is no one option for students with ASD once they leave high school. There are a myriad of options open to adults with ASD, depending on how the disability will affect the adult in postsecondary activities. Whether a young adult goes on to postsecondary education, to get a job, or to participate in a daily activity program depends on the skills he has and the level of independence at which he can use them.

Postsecondary Education

There are several options for young adults with ASD to consider as they explore postsecondary options. The chart on the next page previews the skills and abilities generally needed to benefit from the different types of education.

Gathering information about types of postsecondary programs that may be appropriate for your child, as well as the criteria for specific schools or programs, can be difficult, but here are some ideas:

1. Ask the guidance counselor at school if he or she is aware of any postsecondary programs that might be a good fit for your child.
2. Attend local college fairs and ask the exhibitors whether their institution has disability support services such as tutoring and coaching or a program for students with disabilities.
3. Ask your child's teachers what programs their former students have attended.
4. Call your local ARC or autism support group and ask whether they have a listing of programs in the area or whether they sponsor workshops on postsecondary options.
5. Consult directories of colleges and universities to locate those with programs for students with disabilities.
6. Ask other parents of students with ASD or developmental disabilities to share information about postsecondary options that they are aware of.
7. Visit the website www.thinkcollege.net for information on postsecondary programs for students with intellectual or developmental disabilities.
8. Consult the resources listed under Postsecondary Education in the Resource Guide at the back of the book.

Type of Education: **TRADITIONAL 2-YEAR OR 4-YEAR COLLEGE**

(attending school on a part-time or full-time basis with the goal of earning a degree)

Skills and Abilities Needed	Other Considerations
■ Ability to take entrance assessments and complete application process ■ Academic ability to navigate college-level coursework ■ Ability to advocate for needed accommodations ■ Ability to independently communicate in order to share ideas, ask questions, and solve problems ■ Ability to focus on content and discussions ■ Ability to understand various perspectives	■ Does the student have the self-care, housekeeping, and other skills needed to live independently (or with minimal support) on campus in a dorm or apartment? ■ Can the student socialize appropriately with roommates, classmates, teachers, etc.? ■ Can the student focus on assignments and accept *not being perfect?* ■ Can the student structure time, set priorities, organize work independently or with minimal support?

Type of Education: **VARIATION ON TRADITIONAL**

2-4 year college programs for students with developmental or intellectual disabilities (such programs typically lead to a certificate and can be a bridge to a 2- or 4-year traditional degree program.

Skills and Abilities Needed	Other Considerations
Requirements vary from program to program, but may include: ■ Tested IQ at a certain level ■ Ability to behave appropriately in a classroom or job setting ■ Ability to communicate both expressively and receptively ■ Basic self-help and daily living skills ■ Academic ability or vocational aptitude to benefit from the program of study	■ What are the student's career goals? ■ What type of supports might the student need in order to access education (Accommodations? Education coach?)? ■ Should the student consider dual enrollment while still in a high school setting?

Type of Education: TECHNICAL SCHOOLS

(attending a program designed primarily to prepare graduates for work in a particular field of work such as auto mechanics, graphic design, cosmetology, computers, criminal justice, health care, culinary, hospitality, etc.)

Skills and Abilities Needed	Other Considerations
■ Ability to take entrance assessments and complete application process ■ Academic ability to navigate specialized coursework in chosen field ■ Ability to advocate for needed accommodations ■ Ability to independently communicate in order to share ideas, ask questions, and solve problems ■ Ability to focus on content and discussions ■ Ability to understand various perspectives ■ Ability to understand and balance book work and hands-on activities	■ Can the student socialize appropriately with classmates and instructors? ■ Can the student focus on assignments and accept *not being perfect?* ■ Can the student structure time, set priorities, organize work independently or with minimal support? ■ Can the student use transportation to get to and from school?

Type of Education: REHABILITATION PROGRAMS

(designed to help people with developmental disabilities learn independent living skills and job skills—these are mostly day programs that the student attends while living in the community; programs may be run by state and local departments of vocational rehabilitation or local/private nonprofit agencies)

Skills and Abilities Needed	Other Considerations
■ Ability to communicate basic needs and wants ■ Ability to perform some activities of daily living independently ■ Ability to follow directions with needed supports and accommodations	■ Can the student understand directions and express himself well enough to participate in the program?

Employment Possibilities

Young adults with autism spectrum disorders have been known to do a wide variety of jobs, ranging from unskilled labor to working within highly sophisticated technical professions. The key is to *individualize, individualize, individualize*. Do not allow the diagnostic label of an autism spectrum disorder to limit your vision. At the same time, it is imperative to be realistic in your goals so that you and your child do not waste time pursuing employment that will never be achievable.

There are several broad categories of possible employment settings that you might consider when planning to launch an individual with ASD into the workforce. These include:

1. Competitive employment,
2. Sheltered workshops,
3. Vocational rehabilitation agencies,
4. Recreational/leisure day programs, and
5. Family-generated employment opportunities.

Competitive Employment

Some adults with ASD are able to work in a competitive employment setting, earning the same salary and having the same responsibilities as their neurotypical colleagues. Temple Grandin is perhaps the most renowned individual with autism who has been highly successful in her profession, for she has reportedly designed three-fourths of the cattle chutes used in North America. (See the Resource Guide at the back of this book for various books by Dr. Grandin.) Although this type of professional success is relatively rare, the fact that it occurs at all removes the "glass ceiling" assumed when an ASD diagnosis is present and opens the horizons when contemplating potential employment possibilities.

Individuals with high functioning autism (HFA) or Asperger's disorder who are competitively employed often work in technical fields such as computer repair, data analysis, engineering, or the like. These types of jobs take advantage of the areas of strength that are often seen in individuals with ASDs (e.g., rote memory, analytic assessment of data), while not requiring ability in areas that are traditionally weaker for these individuals (e.g., social/interpersonal skills, customer service diplomacy, etc.) Although these workers may be perceived as a bit "quirky" to their colleagues, their notable productivity and attention to detail often outweighs these concerns.

Even when professional jobs are out of reach for a given individual with an ASD, there are other competitive jobs that can be considered. Many people with ASDs are employed in restaurants or other food service settings because these locations offer a variety of tasks which are rather easy and repetitive. Although people without an ASD may find such tasks boring, many individuals on the autism spectrum actually appreciate the consistency and familiarity of these types of tasks. Similarly, working in an office doing rote paperwork such as filing or data entry, stocking shelves in a store, or re-shelving books in a library are viable options to consider for some individuals.

Regardless of the level of sophistication of a competitive job, it is not uncommon to have job coaches on site, at least initially, to help the adult succeed. The job coach can individualize his or her support according to the person's specific needs. For example, one job coach may model how to perform a work-related task, while another may consult with the employer about making environmental changes that would enhance performance (e.g., creating a cubby within the work area to decrease distractions). Criteria need to be spelled out to delineate when the job coach would no longer be considered necessary (for example, based on level of productivity when working independently, frequency of inappropriate vocalizations, etc.). Until these criteria are consistently met, the job coach should remain on-site (at least part of the time) so that the individual with an ASD is not set up for failure due to inadequate support.

"Sheltered Workshops"

Although the term sheltered workshop has become somewhat antiquated, it is still frequently used to describe employment settings that are set up specifically for adults with developmental disabilities such as autism spectrum disorders. The emphasis in these settings is to provide a location where prevocational and vocational training can occur within a protected, understanding atmosphere. Jobs available in sheltered workshops usually involve basic prevocational practice tasks (e.g., sorting items or simple custodial tasks such as sweeping the floor).

Sheltered workshops often have contracts with local companies to have the workshop employees complete tasks such as packaging, simple assembly, or other rote activities. The local company pays the sheltered workshop on a piecemeal basis, and employees then receive paychecks that are commensurate with their productivity. Although the sum is usually small, the employees have the opportunity to associate their performance with the subsequent positive consequence of a paycheck.

Ideally, for the majority of employees, the sheltered workshop should be a transitional setting where they can learn the fundamental skills necessary before applying to a competitive job. The better workshops have work crews that go into the community, job coaches who can accompany employees when they start a new job outside of the workshop, and other means of helping employees make the transition to a more competitive work environment. At the same time, some individuals with ASDs might need the heightened level of supervision available in a sheltered workshop their entire working careers.

When and whether your adult child will be ready to leave a sheltered workshop is certainly not a decision that you need to make in the initial planning stages. Rather, your child's vocational abilities and needs for support will become apparent with experience and time.

State Vocational Rehabilitation Agencies

All states have government-funded agencies that provide training and support to adults with physical, mental, or developmental disabilities, including people with an ASD. Vocational rehabilitation agencies are best suited for individuals who are not quite ready for competitive employment on their own, but already have the fundamental skills usually taught within a sheltered workshop setting. These agencies seek to support the individuals who would otherwise "fall between the cracks."

Vocational rehabilitation agencies can provide vocational assessments, career guidance, and even temporary job coaching, as warranted. They can teach the individual with an ASD how to fill out an application, interview for a job, understand local employment trends, and explore possible accommodations on the job. The vocational rehabilitation staff can also actively help with the job search by contacting local companies via "cold calling," reviewing the classified ads, and serving as a liaison between the individual with an ASD and the hiring manager.

Many vocational rehabilitation agencies work with employers to set up on-site training, or provide job coaching via a vocational rehabilitation staff member. Employers often receive incentive packages (e.g., tax credits) to motivate them to hire people with ASD or other disabilities. This option can be quite effective for adults with ASDs who have a moderate degree of ability but require some level of support to be successful in the workforce.

Recreational/Leisure Day Programs

For some adolescents and adults with more severe forms of autism spectrum disorders, including some who have intellectual disabilities, paid employment may not be a viable option. In these circumstances, other options that are less pressured or vocationally-oriented need to be considered. Adult day programs that focus on providing an opportunity to learn and experience recreational and leisure skills might be the best alternative. Such programs often are low-key and offer individuals with ASD a place to spend time with friends, go on community outings, and learn basic daily living skills. At times the participants may accompany the staff on vocationally oriented tasks such as delivering "Meals on Wheels" or putting advertisements on doorknobs. Usually, however, the participants rely upon the staff to provide ongoing prompting, and independent performance is not a realistic goal.

It should be stressed that these day programs should not be just "adult day care." The programs should develop treatment plans for each participant that specify individualized goals and strategies for reaching those goals. The ratio of staff to participants is often relatively low and therefore the degree of support and assistance is relatively high compared to the options described above.

Although adults with ASD generally do not "graduate" from these programs into a competitive job or sheltered workshop, day programs prevent the individual from becoming housebound, can result in improved daily living skills, and provide the family with some degree of respite.

Family-Generated Employment Opportunities

Some families may be able to create a viable job for their child with ASD using already-developed networking supports such as friends or neighborhood acquaintances. For example, we know a young man with an ASD, Bill, whose long-standing passion is cars. Fortunately, a close family friend was the owner of a local classic car dealership. When Bill was in his last two years of high school, the family, school staff, and car dealer worked actively with Bill to assess what types of tasks he could perform and enjoy at the dealership. He attended a classroom for students with autism in the mornings, and worked at the dealership with the support of a school-based job coach in the afternoons. By the time he graduated from high school, Bill was ready to work full time since he was well versed with the tasks he needed to complete at the dealership, was comfortable with his coworkers, and was earning a minimum-wage salary.

Another example of a family-generated employment opportunity is the one created for Ellie, a young woman with an ASD. Although Ellie was unable to speak, she was able to follow simple instructions and a familiar routine. One of her favorite activities was watching sporting activities such as baseball and football games. As luck would have it, her uncle worked part time as a referee and proposed that Ellie be his "assistant." She began accompanying him to his refereeing stints, and thoroughly enjoyed rounding up the equipment at the end of the games, holding the flag to designate ten yards at football games, and other relatively easy tasks. Initially, she served as a volunteer; over time, she was able to receive a nominal payment through the refereeing association.

It is worth mentioning that Ellie's employment opportunity was generated through notable effort by her family *after* she had already graduated from high school. Although the school and family had worked hard together to create vocational experiences for Ellie during high school, none was successful beyond a few months. In contrast, the refereeing assistant position was a clear match and has been successful for over three years.

Such "thinking outside the box" can create individualized and successful jobs for adults with autism spectrum disorders who have a variety of skill levels. Also, Ellie's experiences prior to her current job are a notable illustration of the fact that sometimes you may need to try one job, then another, and yet a third, until the best match is discovered. Although this can be frustrating, keep in mind that even neurotypical young men and women entering the workforce often switch jobs as they seek their best option.

Which Job Setting Makes the Most Sense?

In other parts of this book, we describe strategies to help you determine which of these employment options make the most sense for your child (or any given individual with an ASD). In brief, your choices will be guided by:

- Interviews with your child, as well as people who know him well;
- reviews of his educational records, including strengths/ needs outlined in his Individualized Education Program;
- vocational assessments;
- degree of progress on IEP goals;
- job coach feedback; and, frankly,
- a large degree of trial and error.

Our primary theme is to stay open minded, creative, and realistic, and to assume that you will need to change course at least a few times before final decisions are made.

Living Arrangements

Just as with employment options, there are a variety of living arrangements to be considered. These potential settings differ as to the degree of supervision, the staff-to-resident ratio, the number of roommates/housemates, requirements regarding whether or not the resident is employed, etc. Assessing each of these variables will help you determine what kind of living arrangement is the best match for a particular young adult with an ASD. Below are descriptions of some of the more common living options.

Independent Living

Adults with autism spectrum disorders who have mastered self-help skills demonstrate problem-solving abilities and are notably self-directed may be able to live on their own. Although uncommon, every so often a person on the autism spectrum is able to maintain his or her own apartment with only sporadic assistance from family or friends. These individuals tend to feel most comfortable living by themselves rather than trying to manage the social pressures of living with another person.

Rooming with a neurotypical peer may be an option for individuals with ASD who need minor support with more sophisticated tasks such as balancing a checkbook or navigating the city's transportation system. College students are a good choice for such arrangements because they often need housing, are similar in age, and can be less intrusive as compared to a hired "staff." Such an arrangement needs to be handled with sensitivity so that the individual with an ASD does not feel "spied upon" or "babysat." However, we have seen this option work quite well if done insightfully and with sensitivity.

Supervised Apartments

Community agencies often offer the option of supervised apartments. These settings allow residents a notable degree of independence while providing support with activities such as cooking, shopping, budgeting, and housekeeping, as needed. For example, some agencies have a "houseparent" model in which a staff member lives in the same apartment complex as the individuals who have autism spectrum disorders or other disabilities. The residents often live in groups of two to four per apartment. Daily drop-bys or scheduled meetings with staff can assure that the adults with an ASD are given the level of support necessary to live on their own.

Group Homes

Group homes are an option for adults with autism spectrum disorders who require more significant supervision. Most group homes include up to six residents living in a community-based home. Trained staff are available to work with the residents 24 hours a day. Generally, staff work on a shift basis and the staff-to-resident ratio is usually quite high.

Residents of group homes frequently go to a day program or sheltered workshop during the day. In fact, for some agencies, this is a requirement for acceptance to the program. The residents often participate in community activities with staff support on the weekends.

Host Home Families

A relatively newer trend that is gaining popularity is the Host Home option. In this model, one or two adults with an ASD live in a host family's home. The family members who live in the home are trained by community or government agencies to use specialized treatment strategies to help the adult(s) reach specified, individualized goals. The emphasis in these settings is to enhance the individuals' daily living skills within a family-like atmosphere.

Generally, this option is considered when the adult with an ASD requires daily support in order to function well on his own. Sometimes the individual's skills progress to the point where he can live in a supervised apartment, while other times the Host Home may end up being a permanent living arrangement.

Some families are hesitant about considering a Host Home because it seems too "close" to their own family situation, and they feel "guilty" that another family is able to provide for their grown child when they can't. However, choosing such a setting is not an indictment of anyone's parenting skills. Rather, families who choose this option can often get some respite after 21 years or more of supporting their son or daughter with an ASD, and their adult child gets the independence of moving out of the family home. In addition, this option is less expensive than a group home and government funding is therefore more available, and the individual often receives a higher level of attention than he would in more traditional residential settings.

Unique Living Arrangements

Some families are able to create a unique living arrangement for their adult child, incorporating some of the characteristics of other settings. For example, we know of a young man, Peter, who was relatively adept with communication, social, and vocational skills, but had some behavioral challenges that were potentially dangerous to others. As a consequence, his parents and a local agency developed a one-person living arrangement for him in the "in-law apartment" of an existing traditional group home. Peter appreciated having his own living quarters separate from the group home residents, while his family was relieved that Peter had ongoing supervision and assistance in learning anger management skills.

Another example of a unique living solution is reflected in the route taken by a rather wealthy, aging single mother of twin men with autism spectrum disorders. The mother set up a trust fund so that the staff who currently provided assistance to her and her sons in their spacious townhouse would continue to do so once she passed away. The staff were dedicated, nurturing individuals who were open to this arrangement and were therefore willing to "sign on" to the responsibility involved. The mother was content in the knowledge that her sons would be able to remain in their family home, while the staff were thankful for the chance to have guaranteed lifelong employment.

Living at Home

Many adults with an ASD end up living with their parents, at least for the initial phase of adulthood. A major reason is that the limited funding available in the U.S. results in a dearth of residential options, so adults with disabilities are frequently on waiting lists for a prolonged period of time. Any household will be bound to feel stressed when offspring in their twenties or thirties continue to live with their parents. As would be expected, this stress can be exacerbated when the young adult is on the autism spectrum. The parents may feel physically or emotionally exhausted or financially stressed due to the continuing demands on their time and energy. And young adults who continue to live at home usually make less progress in developing independence compared to individuals who "leave the nest" because many parents make minimal demands on them.

Nonetheless, at times there are certain advantages to continuing to live at home, at least for awhile. For example, living at home may be the best option when a young adult with an ASD is beginning a job. It can be especially difficult if the person with an ASD is expected to simultaneously adjust to the changes of going to work *and* moving to a new home. Many families focus initially on gaining employment for their adult child with an ASD, and only begin exploring living arrangements once the job situation is settled. Either process is daunting, so focusing on them sequentially rather than concurrently can be more reasonable for most families. Living at home also allows the person with an ASD additional time to fine tune basic skills, which will be essential once he moves to an alternative housing situation.

Thinking Ahead about Future Living Arrangements

If you are reading this book while your child or student is still in high school, it is important to try to envision now which types of living arrangements may be suitable for him after school. This way you can ensure that his IEP includes appropriate goals for daily living skills such as hygiene, cooking, purchasing, home maintenance/cleaning, and the like. These IEP goals are at least as essential as traditional academic objectives. If a young adult with an ASD cannot successfully accomplish these basic daily living skills independently, his options will be greatly limited.

During the transition period, it is highly recommended that parents and students with autism spectrum disorders visit potential living arrangements in order to obtain a general understanding of the requirements of the various settings, the staffing patterns, typical resident profile, and overall atmosphere. In doing so, you can also find out what kind of waiting lists exist for the various options in your community and start to come up with back-up plans, if need be.

Concluding Comments

Regardless of what postsecondary education, employment, or living arrangement you identify for a given young adult with an ASD, it is vital to individualize your options by being creative and accentuating the person's strengths. Hopefully, the review of options in this chapter will increase your enthusiasm as you begin to narrow down the choices to the optimal path to travel.

2 | The Legal Framework for Transition Planning

Most parents can benefit greatly from assistance in transition planning. In the United States, you and your child are entitled to certain types of assistance by law. In addition, as your child approaches adulthood there are other laws that come into play and can affect transition planning. You probably already know a lot about how some of these laws, such as IDEA and NCLB, apply to younger children. In this chapter we will focus specifically on provisions in federal laws that relate to students who are preparing to make the transition from school to adult life.

Background

Discussing the legal aspects of anything can be daunting. It is no different for parents of students with disabilities who are trying to understand how the educational laws apply to their children. Yet, it is critical to understand the legality of educational services and the rights of students with disabilities as your child is preparing to leave school age programming.

Before we discuss the laws and how they apply to transition services for students with autism spectrum disorders, it is important to understand the interaction of the different levels of regulations that govern education. There are federal laws for educating all students. These laws are meant for all students who are educated in public schools. The federal government has also enacted laws specific to the education of students who are deemed to be eligible for special education services under that law. The government authority that oversees special education federal law is the Office of Special Education Programs (OSEP).

State governments, in turn, are required to adopt regulations to implement the federal laws in their respective states. Each state has a Bureau (or Division) of Special Education to design regulations that further define the requirements for putting the law into practice. States can choose to simply adopt the federal regulations that accompany federal law or they can write more explicit legislation that school districts within that state must follow.

Public school districts within each state must follow the regulations as they design service delivery models and special education programming for their districts. Incorporated within the regulations are due process rights and procedural safeguards for parents of students with disabilities. Such safeguards are meant to provide parents and guardians with a forum that allows them to hold the school districts accountable for providing their children with a free and appropriate public education.

Federal Education Laws

Transition planning is inextricably interwoven with educational planning. This is because most of the laws that include provisions for assistance with transitioning out of school are education laws. To understand what transition assistance is available to you and your child, it is therefore important to have a basic understanding of two major federal laws:

1. The Elementary and Secondary Education Act, also known as No Child Left Behind (NCLB) and
2. The Individuals with Disabilities Education Improvement Act (IDEA)

As families are preparing for students to leave school age programs, it is critical to know and act on the rights that both laws afford the students. Once a student leaves secondary education, there are currently very few entitlements afforded students with disabilities; most especially, students on the autism spectrum.

The No Child Left Behind Act

In 1965, a federal education law known as the Elementary and Secondary Education Act was enacted. The most recent reauthorization of this act is known as No Child Left Behind (NCLB). NCLB provides federal funding for *all* students who are being educated in public schools. In a nutshell, NCLB emphasizes holding schools accountable for what they teach, and expects schools to use research-based teaching methods, to employ highly qualified teachers, and to involve parents in their children's education.

One mandate of the law is that students with disabilities have access to the general education curriculum to the greatest extent possible. This requires that students with disabilities participate in statewide assessments. Each state must write academic standards that students are expected to meet as measured on the statewide as-sessment. NCLB, however, does provide states with the opportunity of developing alternate standards and assessments for the two percent of students in each school system who have the most severe cogni-tive impairments. Using the guidelines provided by the state, the IEP team must determine which assessment is most appropriate for each student with disabilities. Given the diversity of students on the autism spectrum, the type of statewide assessment must be thoughtfully considered for every student. Decision-making considerations will be discussed later in this chapter.

Individuals with Disabilities Education Act (IDEA)

If you have a child on the autism spectrum who has been receiv-ing special education services through the public school system, you are probably familiar with some of the provisions in IDEA that apply to students of all ages. For example, the law requires that all students with disabilities be provided with a free, appropriate education in the least restrictive environment and that an Individualized Education Program (IEP) be developed detailing what they are expected to learn and what special services they will receive to help them meet those goals.

When your child reaches her early teens, it is important to un-derstand the specific provisions in the law that apply to students who will be transitioning out of public school once they graduate or "age out" of high school. Notably, the reauthorization of the Individuals with Disabilities Education Improvement Act in 2004 has given much-needed attention to transition services for students with disabilities. A significant change in the law occurs in the *Definitions Section, 1401.* In that section, transition services are defined as:

"a coordinated set of activities for a child with a disability:
(a) that is designed to be a results-oriented process, that is focused on improving the academic and functional achievement of the child with a disability to facilitate the child's movement from school to post-school activities
(b) is based on the individual child's needs and
(c) includes instruction, related services, community experiences, the development of employment and other post-school adult living objectives." [20 U.S.C. Section 1401(34)]

This definition is meant to bring clarity for IEP teams who are designing the educational programs to support students as they move from school to adulthood.

In August 2006, the United States Department of Education Office of Special Education Programs (OSEP) published the IDEA 2006 Regulations. These regulations provide more explicit explanations and procedures for carrying out the intent of the law. They are a way to hold IEP team members accountable for the outcome-based design and implementation of the educational program for students.

The remaining sections of this chapter will focus on the pragmatics of the law in order to guide parents and professionals as they plan for their children's or students' transition to adulthood.

Practical Realities of IDEA

Assessment of Students with Autism Spectrum Disorders

As your child's IEP team begins to plan for her transition out of school, they will need to conduct assessments to guide their decision-making process and program development. For any student, there is no perfect battery of assessments to help teams gather information about how the student is functioning or will function in the future. However, according to the National Collaborative on Workforce and Disability (NCWD/Youth), assessments should focus on talents, knowledge, skills, interests, values, and aptitudes of each individual.

Tools and strategies should be used to determine information about your child's:

1. Communication Skills
2. Functional Skills or Activities of Daily Living
3. Academic Skills
4. Social and Emotional Regulation Skills

Types of Assessments

Most commercially designed assessments that are specifically designed to measure skills of students on the autism spectrum are designed for younger students. This means that when your child is in high school, she is more likely to be administered tests designed for typically developing students.

Norm-referenced Tests. To evaluate communication and academic skills, your child will likely be given a variety of "norm-referenced" standardized assessments. If an assessment is norm-referenced, that means that the developers of the test administered the test to large numbers of students grouped by age and gender. The test developers then determined what the average scores were for children of different ages and genders, based on test results. Scores on these tests are then reported compared to the "norms" for all test takers. For example, a score might be reported at being at a certain percentile such as the 50th percentile (which would mean it is the same score achieved by the average child taking the test). Scores might also be reported more generally as "average," "below average," or "above average." If a test is standardized, it must be given in exactly the same manner to every child. (For instance, the instructions must be read in exactly the same way each time the test is given.)

For students with ASD who may need to have instructions repeated or rephrased in order for them to understand what is asked, a standardized norm-referenced test may not provide the clearest picture of what the student can do with accommodations and supports. However, such tests may be required for your child to qualify for certain services and programs.

Psychologists can administer norm-referenced standardized assessments, such as a Wechsler Individualized Achievement Test (WIAT), to attain scores in academics and verbal achievement.

Speech-language pathologists also have a number of standardized assessments they can use to assess your child's ability to comprehend and use language.

What is key to understand about these types of norm-referenced tests is that the score does not tell you how many items on the test your child got correct or incorrect. Rather, the score compares your child's performance to the performance of the average child in the general population.

Criterion-referenced Tests. Sometimes a more useful test for pinpointing the strengths and needs of a child with disabilities is a "criterion-referenced" test. These tests evaluate how your child performs on a specific set of skills, such as auditory memory or mathematical computation. These tests do not compare your child with other children. Instead, they show whether or not she has achieved particular skills. For example, a criterion-referenced test of language skills might show whether your child understands how to use verb tenses or what time concepts mean. Criterion-referenced tests can provide a clear picture of the skills your child needs to learn and can therefore be helpful in setting goals and choosing services to help her reach those goals.

Informal Tests. Your child's teachers and therapists can also use a variety of informal means to gather information about her skills. For example, they can complete inventories (checklists) and interview you and your child to collect additional information about her communication, functional, and social and emotional regulation skills. Teachers can also design assessments that relate to specific skills and concepts.

Another very helpful assessment tool is observation. Instructors, psychologists, administrators, and agency personnel can watch the student and write about her skills and abilities completing different kinds of tasks in different environments.

These types of tests are typically given during the reevaluation of the student with ASD every two or three years, or in some cases, more frequently to update present educational levels for IEPs. It is important to note that no one specific assessment will benefit all students with ASD. The IEP teams and, particularly, the school psychologist will need to figure out what information is needed and what tools will best provide answers to questions about the student.

Assistive Technology Assessments. IDEA requires that a student's needs for assistive technology be considered at least annually, at the IEP meeting. Still, assistive technology is often an area that is overlooked for students with autism spectrum disorders. Students who are nonverbal or have difficulty communicating basic needs and wants independently may benefit from augmentative and alternative communication (AAC) devices. Students who have difficulty writing could use adaptive keyboards or computer writing software. The technology options for students with disabilities are growing immensely.

The school speech-language pathologist should be able to assess your child to determine whether she would benefit from AAC, or perhaps refer you to a central office for AAC assessment in your school district. Likewise, the school occupational therapist should be able to assess your child for technology that would help her with fine motor or adaptive skill challenges. Additionally, your school district special education administrators and technology directors, and your state Bureau of Special Education should be able to help you find out where your child can obtain assessments and trial devices and software.

Functional Behavior Assessments. For students who are exhibiting behaviors that may interfere with employment or independence, a functional behavior assessment (FBA) may be completed. The functional behavior assessment is a process for determining the cause or function of a behavior. It involves determining what happens before a problem behavior (the "antecedent"), as well as what the person receives as a consequence of her behavior. For example, does she get out of doing a task she does not enjoy? Does she get attention from other students? Is she given a particular item she wants in order to get her to calm down?

Information from an FBA helps IEP teams determine interventions that could be used to teach the student how to get what she wants more appropriately, thereby minimizing or extinguishing the problem behavior. (For more information on FBAs, you may wish to consult *Functional Behavioral Assessments for People with Autism* by Beth Glasberg.)

Performance-based Assessments. A performance-based assessment consists of a task or set of tasks which a student must actually complete to demonstrate her skill and aptitude for the task(s). Performance-based assessments conducted by agencies or school personnel will provide the IEP team with information about your child's needs for training or additional education, her prospects for employment, her independent living skills, and her vocational abilities. These tests are often conducted by local vocational rehabilitation centers or career centers. Sometimes, staff from these centers will even come to the school to assess students and consult with teams. An occupational therapist would also be able to assist with assessing your child's vocational skills and choosing goals and strategies to help her achieve needed skills.

Interest Tests. Interest tests may be the most beneficial in helping a student determine what she is most passionate about. Taking an interest test is often the first step in helping a person find the best match for an occupation or career. These tests are typically in a multiple-choice format and require the ability to select from a list of preferred activities.

Your child's high school counselor can tell you whether interest testing is available in your school district. Also, local rehabilitation agencies or career centers often have computerized interest inventories that are computer scored and provide the user with a printout of the best occupational matches for the student's passions.

The Right Tests for Your Child

Using a varied selection of assessment tools early in your child's high school career can have many benefits for her:

- It can help the IEP team to narrow or widen the scope of post-school opportunities being considered for your child.
- Assessment data can validate or refute the impression that your family and school staff have of your child's skills at a given time.
- The information provided by assessments can give your child's team ideas of instructional areas to focus on and related services to provide.
- Sometimes assessment data reveals the need to reexamine the goals that the IEP team has previously set for your child.

Refer to Chapter 4 for more specific information about questions that assessments may answer during various stages of transition planning.

IEPs for Students with ASD

Simply stated, if the local education agency (LEA)/school district is not providing transition services for the student with ASD as defined on page 26, transition services are not being provided. IDEA *requires* that IEP teams must begin to consider transition services when a student reaches age 16, or earlier if the IEP team deems this appropriate. Also, some states require that transition planning begin at age 14, and since that is a more rigid requirement, it supercedes the federal requirement. Refer to your state's special education regulations.

Although 16 is the *magic transition age*, the effective team incorporates transition services into the annual IEP during the year in which the student will turn 16. The highly effective team will begin to incorporate services in the middle school IEP. As alluded to earlier, it is never too early to start planning for life beyond school, particularly for students with autism spectrum disorders.

Changing Focus

The most significant difference between IEPs for students under age 16 (or 14) and those who have reached transition age is that the IEP now focuses on what we expect the student to know and be able to do once she leaves school. The IEP team needs to move from simply considering the needs of the student as they relate to the current home, school, and community environments to concentrating on designing an educational program that will lead to independence at home and in the community after graduation.

Creating a vision for what life will look like for students after they leave high school is a key component to following the law as it is intended. Activities that IDEA requires IEP teams to explore include:

1. post-secondary education,
2. vocational training,
3. employment,
4. adult services,
5. independent living, and
6. community participation.

Daily living skills and functional vocational evaluations can be incorporated as well. Let's face it, all children dream about what they want to be when they grow up. Then, they change their minds several times before settling in on their first attempt at life after school. Students with ASD need their support systems to assist them in creating their dreams and to contrive learning opportunities that will help them attain their goals along the way. The special education laws give us the framework for doing just that.

To assist IEP teams with following the regulations that are outlined for them, each state develops its own IEP forms and formats. These papers are meant to guide the team as they develop the plan for the student. As a parent once said, the papers are only as good as how what is written on them is carried out in the classroom. She was exactly correct! Teams can put anything that they want on paper. Actually designing the program and then implementing it so a student makes meaningful progress is what counts. Fortunately, IDEA requires that progress be measured frequently and requires an annual review of IEPs for students with disabilities. The most appropriate and functional IEPs are those that are reviewed and revised regularly based on the data that are collected.

Statement of Transition Services

Beginning at age 16, or earlier, the IEP must contain a *statement of transition services* for the student:

- It describes the curriculum that the student will access and participate in to attain her transition goals.
- It lists the coordinated set of activities, together with measurable outcomes, that will enable the student to move from school to post-school activities.
- When appropriate, this statement should include the interagency responsibilities—that is, which agency such as a mental health or vocational agency is going to take on which role(s) and responsibilities.

Here are a few examples of transition statements for students with ASD:

J. is currently 17 years of age and is a junior in his local high school. He is included in the general education curriculum for all of his coursework and requires direct instruction in pragmatic language. J. is interested in pursuing a career in computers; preferably in video game design. He would like to attend the local technical school and continue to live at home with his parents.

*T. is 14 years old and is in the eighth grade at Central
Middle School. She enjoys music and singing. She also likes
playing dress-up with her older sister. T. is currently in a
full-time autistic support program in her neighborhood
school. T.'s parents state that they have not thought much
about T.'s life after school and are interested in doing person-centered planning.*

*N. is a 20-year-old student in a center-based autism class for
students with behavior difficulties. He has one more year of
school. N. is able to complete activities of daily living related
to grooming and hygiene with picture prompts. His self-inju-
rious behaviors have decreased, allowing him to participate
in individual work activities for 15 minutes at a time with
5-minute sensory breaks. He will attend the rehabilitation
service program 2 days per week and will begin transition
into a group home during the second quarter of this IEP.*

The remaining sections of the IEP should all link to the statement
of transition services. For example:

- **Present education levels** of your child should be measured and based on the path that she needs to take to
  achieve her life outcomes. The transition goal and life
  outcomes for a student will dictate what types of skills
  are necessary for her. Using that information, the IEP
  team needs to determine which assessments to give your
  child so they can determine her current skill level and the
  starting point for instruction. For example, if a student is
  going to enter a tech school for auto mechanics, he or she
  must be proficient in algebra and geometry. Assessments
  in those areas will help the team determine what courses
  are needed in high school in order for the student to enter
  the program upon graduation.

- The **goals and objectives** in each identified instructional
  area must correspond to the transition needs that are
  identified as next steps in the present education levels.
  Continuing the example from the paragraph above, the
  goal for the student may read, "Using an alternate cur-

riculum and calculator, C. will demonstrate proficiency in the essential concepts of Algebra 2 as outlined in the course syllabus by earning a 75% or higher."

- **Specially designed instruction** should be selected and identified so that your child can make meaningful progress. Later on, the instructional methods and practices used with your child should be revised based on progress monitoring data.

- **Related supports and services** should include therapies and services that will assist your child in developing independence as well as allowing her to benefit from instruction. These services are the same as those provided to younger students receiving special education services, including speech and language therapy, physical and occupational therapy, counseling, etc. The focus of the services, however, must be related to the student's transition goals and life outcomes. Therefore, the types of services provided to a given student may change from those that will help her succeed in an educational setting to those that will help her develop skills for an employment setting. For example, a student may not have qualified for occupational therapy when younger if she could write well enough to complete school assignments. But if she needs to develop fine motor skills to enable her to meet her transition goal of learning keyboarding skills, then she may qualify for OT.

- **The educational setting** where your child will receive instruction and services should also be linked to the statement of transition services. Knowing that IDEA supports inclusive practices for students with disabilities, the IEP teams for students with ASD must strategically consider whether it is in the student's best interests to be included in general education classes. For example, the team would probably decide that a student who is working towards a regular high school diploma and has the transition goal of attending college should participate in general education classes. On the other hand, the team might decide that a student who is working toward a supported employment option may not benefit from the tenth grade music history class, but might be better served by getting hands-on work experience in vocational classes or through a work-study program. Again, participation in the general education curriculum should link directly to the transition plan.

Monitoring Progress

IDEA requires that progress toward goals on the IEP be reviewed as often as the progress of a student in the general education setting. This means you should receive quarterly reports about your child's progress towards her goals. When students are beginning the phases of transition (see Chapter 4), teams may determine that it is beneficial to meet monthly to review progress and make necessary revisions. This will help for two reasons:

1. If this student is not on track and revisions need to be made, she will not go for a long period of time being frustrated or working on needless skills.
2. Once a student begins the transition process, more people will be part of the IEP team. More frequent progress meetings can provide time for everyone who is working on the transition plan with the student to make sure that the comprehensive plan is on track and that services are not being needlessly duplicated.

Meetings to discuss your child's progress should be written into the IEP under the Supports for School Personnel or Specially Designed Instruction sections.

Keeping the End in Sight

When considering life outcomes for students with ASD, no matter what age that process begins, teams have the obligation to start with a discussion of where they see the child in the future. Teams need to consider academic, communication, and socialization skills (the first three areas that are typically reviewed). Also, and arguably more importantly, they should also consider skills that the student will need to function in society as independently as she possibly can. Once a vision is established as discussed in Chapter 1, the team can step backwards in time to the present and create benchmarks along the way. They can review resources such as standards and evidenced-based curricula and methods to incorporate into specially designed instruction for the student as well as related services and supports that the student will need to develop independence.

Sounds great, doesn't it? As terrific as it sounds, this is hard and emotional work. Often parents, realizing that their students can stay in public education until they turn 21, try to put off looking so far ahead. They are overwhelmed by the day-to-day activities needed to support their child with ASD **today,** let alone trying to think about their child's life seven to nine years from now. Not to mention that parents are well aware that we continue to learn about autism treatments and it can be hard not to hope that perhaps one will be developed that will help or even cure *my child*.

As much as living in the moment makes sense, IEP teams who begin to think about life after school as early as possible provide the student with the most valuable education possible. Educators, parents, and advocates must collaborate to create a balance between living in the here and now and planning for the future. The statutes in IDEA are designed to provide the road map to the future.

Other Laws That Affect Transition Planning

Guardianship Laws

Once they reach the age of majority, students with autism spectrum disorders are legally adults. Like other adults, they are entitled to make their own educational and medical decisions and enter into legally binding contracts—unless a guardian is appointed to make some or all of those decisions for them. At least one year before the

---

Changing Focus

Currently, the age of majority is 18 in all states and the District of Columbia except that it is:
- Age 19, in Alabama and Nebraska
- Age 21, in Colorado, Mississippi, and Pennsylvania

(P.W.D. Wright and P.D. Wright, 2007)

student reaches the age of majority, it is therefore recommended that parents and guardians seek the advice of an attorney to determine whether it would be wise to consider guardianship. It is critical that guardianship decisions are based on the best interests of the child and that the least restrictive alternative of guardianship be selected in order to preserve the rights and dignity of the student with ASD or developmental disabilities.

Transfer of IDEA Rights for Students with ASD

Once a student reaches the age of majority, rights that were once held exclusively by the parents can now be legally exercised by the adult student. This does not mean, however, that the student has exclusive rights to oversee her education. Rather, all invitations, procedural safeguards notices, copies of reports, etc., must be given to both the student and the parent of the student with ASD. Parents can continue to attend all meetings where decisions about the student's program and placement will be made if the student chooses to have the parents present or if the parents have legal guardianship of the student.

The intent of the Transfer of Rights in IDEA is that a student will play a more active role in her educational program decisions. Because some students may not be ready to take on that responsibility at the age of 18 (or 19 or 21, depending on your state), IDEA requires that parents be notified one year before rights will transfer to their child. That gives parents and IEP team members an opportunity to discuss whether transferring rights is in the student's best interests. If so, they can prepare her for the transfer of rights. If not, the parents can consider either:

1. being named their child's guardian when she reaches the age of majority, or
2. asking their child to either formally delegate educational decisions to them, in writing, or reaching an informal agreement with her to allow them to continue to be involved in educational decision making.

If neither of these actions is taken, parents will have to rely solely on the student's report of how education is going. They will not have the right to ask questions or make decisions on the student's behalf. (The same holds true if the student goes on to postsecondary education. Parents do not have a right to see educational records, report cards, etc. or participate in educational planning unless they are appointed their child's guardian or have reached an agreement with her as in #2, above.)

Here are some examples of reasons it may not be in the best interests of a student with ASD to take over decision making about her own education:

- The literal-thinking student with ASD may be able to interpret factual concepts related to educational decisions but may not have the skills to infer the consequences for such decisions in the future. For example, the student may select accommodations such as pass/fail grading without asking how the credits will be assigned for that class. Or she may not advocate for a testing accommodation that she needs in order to succeed in a class. As a result, the student may not achieve the number of credits needed to graduate or may fail to achieve the grade point average needed for admission to a postsecondary program.
- A student may assume that she will be able to attend a community college with an instructional assistant for support and may not understand that such a support will not be available once she graduates from high school.
- A student with ASD may apply for and get a job in competitive employment that requires her to work weekends and evenings. She may not realize that the school will only provide her with a job coach during school hours.

Leading up to the decision as to whether to transfer rights to a particular student at the age of majority, the IEP team must be teaching that student how to advocate for herself. This process is described more specifically in Chapter 4 when creating independence is discussed.

The Rehabilitation Act of 1973

While IDEA provides specific entitlements to students receiving special education in public schools, there are no such laws once a student leaves high school. The next best thing to IDEA for students in postsecondary education are the rights afforded by Section 504 of the Rehabilitation Act of 1973 (amended in 1992 and 1998). This section of the law makes it illegal for any program receiving federal funding to discriminate against anyone with a disability. Since most colleges, technical schools, and trade schools receive at least some federal funds, they are required to provide reasonable accommodations for the student with disabilities.

Reasonable accommodations under Section 504 can include: taped books, readers or scribes, notetakers, access to the instructor's notes, extended time for assignments and tests, the use of a calculator, preferential seating, or the like. Section 504 does not require that a written plan be developed for the student, although many postsecondary programs do put a student's accommodations in writing.

To receive any accommodations under Section 504, the student or her advocate must request them. The fact that a student had services in a high school setting does not ensure that she will be able to have accommodations in a postsecondary setting. However, if a student has psychological testing that indicates she has a disability and can furnish IEPs showing the accommodations she received in high school, most colleges and technical schools will provide similar accommodations.

The Rehabilitation Act regulates vocational rehabilitation in every state. Each state has rehabilitation services for people with disabilities to help them get the job training and support they need to become productive members of society. The website www.disabilityinfo.gov has a list of links to state offices. The services available through vocational rehabilitation agencies are the next best thing to IDEA for people with disabilities who have graduated and are seeking support in the workforce.

Other Considerations for the Transition Team

IDEA assists families with some aspects of planning for the future of their child with ASD, yet there are other facets outside of the education arena that families must also address. The following are other important considerations:

Legal Issues

Consulting an attorney to assist your family with specific lifestyle decisions is the best option to ensure that all aspects of legal planning are addressed. Many families of individuals with ASD find it helpful to get legal advice about the following issues:

Irrevocable Special Needs Trust. This document is the most commonly used estate planning tool to protect the financial benefits of the person with disabilities. After the parents' deaths, a special needs trust ensures that funds left to the individual are used for her benefit, rather than being used for care that would otherwise be funded by federal programs such as Medicare or Supplemental Security Income (SSI). It also ensures that the person's assets do not increase to the point that she is disqualified from receiving need-based government benefits.

Power of Attorney. This document establishes who will make decisions on behalf of the person with disabilities in the event she is unable to make such decisions on her own. Powers of Attorney can be made very specific so they just cover instances where the individual needs assistance with making decisions in particular areas, such as with medical care or financial issues.

Letter of Intent. This document, although not legally binding, allows the family to state their wishes related to what kind of life they envision for their child. Then, in the event of the death or incapacitation of the parents, the Letter of Intent can be used to guide others in choosing living arrangements, continued education, employment, social activities, religious affiliation, medical care, behavior management, advocacy, trustees, and final arrangements.

Financial Issues

A financial planner can assist your family with decisions about how to invest assets on behalf of your child with ASD—without compromising her eligibility for government benefits. This person can assist with resources as they relate to government benefits such as SSI, Social Security Disability Insurance (SSDI), Medicaid, and Medicare.

It is beyond the scope of this book to go into further detail about legal and financial issues related to transition planning for your child. The Resource Guide at the back of this book, however, lists publications and organizations that can support you in these areas.

Concluding Comments

The most important aspect of planning for the future of an individual with an ASD is that everyone who is providing advice about any given area should be aware of what the other people are recommending. Coordinating efforts will lead to the development of a comprehensive, individualized plan, and, hopefully, help to avoid future family conflict.

3 | Creating an Effective Transition Team

Much like a coach assembling a winning team, parents and caregivers need to know the abilities and limitations of the individuals or agencies involved in the transition process. That way they can decide who is going to be able to help them get to where they want to go even if they only know the *general* direction of the destination. This chapter will discuss the process of assembling a dynamic and effective transition team for a student with autism, and outline strategies for keeping the team responsive to the student's changing needs while staying committed to the goal of creating a positive result for him.

As mentioned in Chapter 2, during the transition years a student's IEP must include specific transition services as defined by the Individuals with Disabilities Education Improvement Act of 2004 (IDEA). These transition services must align with a course for the student's future, a course that reflects his or her choices, preferences, and needs in the areas of:

- education and training,
- employment,
- adult living arrangements, and
- community experiences.

Parent and student involvement in all aspects of transition planning is a requirement of IDEA, and educators and community service providers must collaborate effectively with families to help students achieve their goals. That said, it is sometimes difficult to identify who will be responsible for ensuring that the process is moving along in a timely and effective manner. For many students, the consistent overseer is the family, often with the support of a few trusted friends and professionals. The Local Education Agency (LEA) will initiate the process as dictated by federal regulations, but education and agency personnel change. Therefore, it is important that the school team knows that the family is overseeing the process.

The actual transition process is relatively straightforward:

1. Decide what you need to know and do;
2. Enlist a few trusted friends and professionals to help identify additional supports and services;
3. Meet to create action plans with due dates; and
4. Hold people accountable for following through on the steps.

Keeping the makeup of the team flexible and responsive to your child's changing needs, and ensuring that the appropriate individuals are included at the most opportune times in the process, is one key to effective planning. The nature of the transition process calls for the involvement of a variety of people including agencies, educators, and advocates, just to name a few. Coordinating so many people from so many different fields can be unwieldy unless certain planning tools are used.

Fortunately, a variety of planning tools have been developed to help teams define a direction for transition, achieve consensus, and follow through on implementation. Two of the more helpful strategies include:

1. Creating a visual or graphic representation of the process for easy and frequent reference (there is a transition portfolio planning tool in Chapter 7 that you can use for this purpose); and
2. Using *person-centered planning* (see the sidebar on the next page for a brief discussion).

Regardless of which planning format your child's team chooses, you can use the subsequent plan to assess the team's progress and to ascertain how closely the team is following the agreed-upon directions. One of the most challenging aspects of this type of process is knowing when to keep to the plan and when to be flexible as your child's needs and abilities change. However, these tools provide an overall framework, and the resultant written plan can be a way for new team members to get up to speed quickly and to clarify their part in the process.

What Is Person Centered Planning?

Various "person centered" frameworks for transition planning have been developed through the years. The goal within these formats is to emphasize the individual's strengths, preferences, capabilities, and positive experiences as a template to creating a vision for his future. Typically, a group of people from diverse backgrounds who have known or worked with the individual for some time meet with him and his family to develop a written plan. Goals are chosen for the person, and tasks that are needed to help the person achieve those goals are assigned to specific team members. Examples of these person-centered frameworks include PATH (Planning Alternative Tomorrows with Hope) as developed by Jack Pearpoint, John O'Brien, and Marsha Forest (1993) and MAPS (Making Action Plans) created by Marsha Forest and Evelyn Lusthaus (1990).

One of the fundamental axioms of these approaches is that the plan should be centered on the person with a developmental disability, rather than being limited by what the "system" has to offer. Team members attempt to involve the person with a disability in the planning process and to determine what his interests, abilities, and preferences are related to employment, living arrangements, and recreational activities. As a consequence, plans are often remarkably creative, individualized, and sensitive to the specific individual's wishes. For additional information, please refer to the References.

Makeup of the Transition Team

During the majority of a student's educational career, the IEP team is comprised of parents plus education and related service personnel. As the student enters adolescence, the IEP team takes on transition as a primary focus, and the members of the team may change as a result. The team needs to expand to include the larger community, and is reflective of the need for the student's educational program, or course of study, to expand into the larger community as well. The IEP team members who are most relevant to the transition team can become a working subcommittee of the IEP team, often meeting on their own to focus specifically upon issues specific to post-school goals and objectives.

The critical members of this IEP Transition team include:

- the student with as ASD and his family or guardians,
- advocates for the student and family,
- school personnel such as special educators,
- counselors,
- transition specialists,
- department supervisors,
- vocational rehabilitation counselors, and
- adult service agency representatives.

Depending on the needs of each student with autism, the team may also include behavior specialists, mental health professionals, related service providers (e.g., speech, physical, or occupational therapists), job trainers, and any other person who is invited to attend by the parent or guardian.

It is important for you to have a discussion with your local school district or local education agency (LEA) to compile a complete list of who should be invited to IEP meetings during the transition process. Although there are legal guidelines that define who must be invited to participate in the transition process, parents or guardians can identify anyone else that they feel would be a valuable member of the group and include them in the invitation list. Before each IEP meeting, it is usually best practice to discuss with the teacher or case manager which members are essential participants if a specific issue is expected to be addressed. This assures that important information is dispersed to the relevant IEP members so that the transition process can continue smoothly.

Each member of the transition team must have a vested interest in the transition outcome for your child. It is essential that the people involved in the planning and implementation of the program are knowledgeable in the field of autism and are invested in learning about your child's individual characteristics. Not all team members need to be experts in autism per se, but they do need at least a basic understanding and knowledge of this disorder, as well as a commitment to think outside the confines of traditional structures and systems. At the very least, all of the professionals who work with your child must be familiar with the accommodations, modifications, and supports that are stated in his IEP as being necessary for him to achieve his goals during transition.

Possible Team Members

The student with autism is obviously the most important member of the transition team. As outlined in Chapters One and Five, the degree to which a given student with autism can actively participate varies widely depending on his abilities. Regardless of your child's skill level, however, it is essential that he be as involved as possible throughout the transition process. If his skill level limits his participation, all IEP transition team members must be sure to communicate updated information regarding his preferences and abilities to one another. (Please see Chapter Five for specific techniques that can enhance a student's participation during the transition process.)

The parents and/or guardian(s) are usually the most constant factor throughout the transition process from school to young adulthood. They know their child better than anyone else at the table and can provide information critical to developing a comprehensive plan. It is the family who knows and lives with the child in the world where he or she will be living as an adult—the world of home, church, neighborhood, doctor's offices, leisure activities, and transportation. Your input is therefore critical in providing a complete and accurate picture, from which the team builds the transition goals and objectives. You can provide a far deeper understanding of your child than any staff members from school or human service agencies can, no matter how well meaning the people with those agencies may be.

Educational staff (especially teachers) are the transition team members primarily responsible for gathering information, communicating with the team members, coordinating school-related services, and planning and providing instruction. They also collect and reflect on the progress monitoring data, suggest adjustments in the instructional program as needed, communicate these adjustments to the parents and other team members, and then put it all together into a draft IEP document that the team can use to develop the final transition plan. *The importance of teacher and parent communication cannot be overstated.* The relationship between the parent and the teacher can provide the vehicle to merge the world of school and the outside world.

In addition to teachers, IDEA also requires that transition teams include a representative from the school district who is qualified to supervise the provision of specially designed instruction the child requires in order to learn effectively. This person is usually at an administrative level, knowledgeable about the general education curriculum, and responsible for allocating the resources necessary to fulfill the IEP. Finally, if specific evaluations for your child are being conducted and discussed, then an educational professional who can interpret the evaluation results is also required to be in attendance (e.g., a psychologist to review the scores on an intelligence test).

Community agencies can supply many possible members of the IEP transition team. Agencies may represent a variety of postsecondary service options, including:

- **Vocational rehabilitation:** Vocational Rehabilitation agencies may be able to conduct formal assessments of a student's employability and suggest jobs that would be a good match. These agencies can also help workers find supportive employment opportunities such as community-based jobs and provide or arrange for needed supports such as job coaches.

- **Residential facilities:** Representatives from group homes, supervised apartments, etc. may attend your child's meetings to begin to get to know him, as well as to provide updated information regarding funding and housing programs in the community.

- **Mental health support:** Community agencies specializing in mental health services may be asked to attend transition meetings in order to support students who have emotional or behavioral concerns that might complicate a successful transition to work or community living come adulthood. These team members can help assure a smooth transition by linking the individual with local mental health providers such as counselors or psychiatrists (if medications are prescribed).

- **County case managers:** Most individuals with autism spectrum disorders are eligible for case management services from their local county agency, identified by their county of residence. These case managers/service coordinators are knowledgeable about services that are available within the county and can also serve as the family's advocate at meetings. The agency name differs from state to state (for example, in Pennsylvania the Department of Mental Health/Mental Retardation provides this service;

in New Jersey the relevant state department is entitled
the Division of Developmental Disabilities). You will need
to investigate the name of the county-funded agency in
your own particular state of residence.

■ **Day program providers:** If plans for your child do not
include looking for competitive employment or pursuing
additional education after high school graduation, his
team might want to consider a day program for him, such
as a sheltered workshop or an adult recreational program.

Trying to sort out which community agencies might be helpful
can be confusing, as there are a myriad of agencies available across
communities and they each can have different names, criteria for
eligibility, and funding options. Many have waiting lists and the
procedures used by each adult service provider are often different.
This is why there are many committees and special task force teams
across the country working on integrating this maze of service providers into a coordinated and accessible system. For now, however,
some of the people who can be helpful in deciding what agencies to
invite include the school social worker or guidance counselor, a case
manager from your given state's department supporting individuals
with autism, local advocates, and parent support groups. Try to include
representatives from these agencies as early as possible to facilitate
a smooth transition.

During the initial long-range planning process for your child,
you can focus on merely identifying the agencies that could be relevant to your child's needs. For example, at an early transition IEP
meeting, one team member may be assigned the task of contacting
agencies for initial information that can then be shared with the rest
of the transition team.

When an agency is listed on the IEP, and is designated to perform
a transition service to which they agreed, they are responsible for providing that service according to IDEA. If an agency fails to provide the
service, then the school is responsible for calling a team meeting to
create an alternate plan to meet the objectives set forth in the IEP.

Other people who can be invited to be part of the transition team
include anyone with special knowledge or expertise regarding your
child with autism or regarding autism in general. According to IDEA,
parents, the student, and the school are free to invite whomever they

choose to the IEP meeting, although it is helpful to share the names and roles of a new member with other team members ahead of time. That way everyone is aware of potential changes in roles, strategies, or goals for the student with autism.

Breakout Groups are often created within transition teams. These subgroups are a means of promoting efficient use of everyone's time. Each breakout group can be assigned a particular area within the transition plan. For example, the parents and a parent advocate could gather information about recreational activities, while the job trainer and county case manager could collect names of potential work settings. Afterwards, each breakout group can share their results with the rest of the transition team, and the team as a whole can create appropriate transition goals.

Determining Roles and Responsibilities for Each Transition Team Member

In order to identify the specific roles and responsibilities for each team member, let's first look at the various activities that take place during the transition process. The IEP transition team generally engages in three activities:

1. It reviews appropriate post-education options;
2. It designs creative educational programs to address the student's unique needs, including identifying instructional activities to assure a meaningful sequence of skills and abilities; and
3. It collects progress-monitoring data on an ongoing basis, making modifications in the plan as warranted by the data and changing circumstances.

Let's briefly describe each of these activities here. More detail on these activities is provided in Chapter 4.

Reviewing Post-High School Options

The first decision that needs to be made is whether your child with an ASD will go straight to work when he graduates from high school, or will continue his education. If continuing education past high school is deemed inappropriate, there are a wide variety of possible work options that can be considered, ranging from competitive employment to working in a sheltered workshop setting. If your child can be successful in a secondary education setting such as a university, then decisions need to be made regarding the intensity of the program (e.g., two-year versus four-year program, local versus farther from home), as well as the chosen area of study.

Of course, the types of employment or secondary education options that are considered for a particular student depend upon the level of supervision that he will require, whether he has any challenging behaviors, and his individual preferences. While some students with ASDs are able to go on to college, others remain full-time in the special education system until age 21 and then graduate to a supportive employment setting. Others attend high school classes on a part-time basis and spend the rest of the week working in the community during the last year or two of public education.

It is important to note that the intellectual or academic abilities of a given individual do not always provide a clear indication as to whether attending college is the best path. For example, although some individuals with high functioning autism (HFA) or Asperger's disorder can have notable academic skills or obtain exceptional SAT scores, their limited social skills and organizational gaps may make attending college overly ambitious. It is important for parents and professionals to either help the student overcome these deficits, or explore other routes such as vocational schools. Otherwise, it can be highly stressful for someone with an ASD to try to cope with the social and organizational demands of a college atmosphere.

Designing Creative Educational Programs

It is often necessary to "think outside the box" when developing a transition program for a student with an ASD. A major reason is that it is common for these individuals to have a wide range of skills across skill areas. For example, someone with an ASD might have notable skills in art but severely limited social skills. Also, students with ASD tend to have idiosyncratic characteristics such as sensory issues or passions that need to be considered. As you might expect, *creativity and individualization* are the keys to success.

Once the IEP transition goals are identified for your child, the members of the team need to specify the specially designed instruction (SDI) your child needs in order to reach these goals. These might include one-to-one teaching, visual supports, behavioral plans, etc. That is, SDI consists of any instructional techniques that would not typically be part of a student's general or special education protocol.

When designing the educational program, keep in mind that IEP goals must be taught in a clear, rational sequence. Make sure that precursor skills are taught before your child moves on to more advanced skills. For example, your child needs to learn the sequence of the alphabet before he can learn to file papers alphabetically; he needs to have basic social behaviors such as making eye contact before he can practice interview skills. Timing is also important. For example, if you anticipate that it might take some time for your child to learn a given skill, make sure it is included in earlier IEPs. Conversely, if a given skill will be relatively easy for your child to

---

The Job Trainer's Role

Since the job trainer is a relatively new member of the IEP team who enters the scene during transition, let's review this person's role and responsibilities. Most school systems hire special education teachers to serve as job trainers to support students with disabilities, starting at approximately age sixteen.

Although the specific details of the job trainer's role vary from state to state (and even from county to county within a state), there are a few general themes that are consistent. In addition to collecting data as noted above, the job trainer provides support to students within the job setting, serves as a liaison between the educational and work staff, and implements any job-related instruction listed on the IEP. In addition, it is the job trainer's responsibility to make sure that the specially designed instructional techniques (SDIs) that have proven effective for a student in the classroom (e.g., picture schedules, modeling, etc.) are adapted and used in the community setting.

Job trainers are usually assigned to a student with an ASD when community-based employment is being considered. Most students on the autism spectrum would find it difficult to succeed in a community-based job without some level of on-site support (at least initially); therefore, the job trainer can be essential in providing

learn but he will only need it once he is out of high school (e.g., filling out a job application), wait until closer to graduation before adding this goal to the IEP.

Collecting Data and Progress Monitoring

It is critical that progress monitoring data be gathered throughout the transition process. Consistently collecting data about your child's progress on IEP goals will provide ongoing and immediate feedback on the effectiveness of his transition plan. By analyzing the data, you and your child's team will know whether modifications need to be made to assure your child continues to make progress toward a successful transition.

Collecting and assessing data is a time-consuming process and cannot be left solely to one IEP team member, such as the class-

---

this type of assistance. Often, the job trainer's involvement begins with an in-class assessment of the student's strengths/needs, learning characteristics, and job preferences, followed by a meeting to discuss this information with the IEP team. The job trainer also develops relationships with local employers who are willing to hire students with autism and other developmental differences, and can recommend these sites as possible placements for the student.

At your child's IEP meeting, already-identified employment settings and other possible community-based sites will be discussed and one or two will be chosen for your child to try. For example, students may be taken to work at a local pizza parlor, retail store, or landscaping business. These experiences are usually seen as experimental in nature rather than permanent job placements. They provide your child and IEP team members with invaluable information regarding his job potential and future directions that may be warranted.

The job trainer needs to be well acquainted with your child's IEP goals and specially designed instructions. He or she should be provided with a copy of your child's IEP with relevant areas highlighted. The job trainer is mandated to follow the guidelines as listed in the IEP. For example, if your child requires written guidelines to complete vocational activities, the job trainer could create a list of the tasks involved in a given job.

room teacher. Related service personnel such as job trainers often work with transitioning students on a regular basis outside of the classroom; therefore, they should be participants in the progress monitoring process as well. These professionals look at the student through a different lens than the teacher does and can provide valuable insight into what work-related skills need to be reinforced or taught. Also, as has been shown repeatedly in the research literature, individuals with autism tend to have difficulties generalizing newly acquired skills across people, settings, and materials. Therefore, data collected by job trainers are especially useful in determining how well the student is generalizing the skills learned in the classroom to the community.

Role Release

When students in special education are younger, each IEP member has specific roles and responsibilities that are relatively clear-cut and consistent. The teacher develops academic goals, the speech-language therapist addresses communication issues, etc. During the transition years, however, professionals need to stretch their roles from supporting a student in the relatively controlled setting of a classroom to helping students acquire and practice skills in the less regimented community setting. Sometimes this can result in accidental fragmentation of team efforts. However, stepping out of traditional responsibilities with a strategy such as *role release* can help to foster team cohesiveness.

Role release refers to the practice of IEP team members stepping outside of their typical roles, or set of duties, and using their unique perspective to look at another area of instruction. For example, the teacher could go into the community with a job trainer and collaborate with the trainer on developing specially designed instruction for your child that would make sense in the community setting. The teacher can then create classroom lesson plans that will help your child achieve his community-related goals. This same type of cross-discipline teamwork can be used by other transition team members such as speech-language therapists, occupational therapists, family members, and psychologists.

Although teachers are ultimately responsible for making sure that IEP activities are completed, students can make more progress when all team members collaborate with the teachers. It is therefore imperative that team members work closely with the teacher to assist in teaching and reinforcing skills in many different settings with a variety of people. This is especially true for individuals with ASDs, since they tend not to generalize skills spontaneously across settings, people, or materials.

Auxiliary Transition Team Members

Sometimes it is beneficial to include people outside of the educational system on a given student's transition team. For example, a given student's team might include agency advocates, older siblings, extended family members, neighbors, or community business owners, etc.

These new team members can often provide a fresh perspective to the transition process because they have not been so entrenched in the educational system. They might know people in the community who can help to facilitate a smooth transition for the student with an ASD (e.g., someone who might employ the student), and can sometimes offer insights as to whether or not a given plan is truly realistic. More than one transition plan has been revised once an auxiliary member has provided an objective reality check!

If you choose to include auxiliary members on your child's IEP transition team, make sure they are clearly committed to your child's successful launching from high school to the community. The transition process can demand a great deal of effort and time across a period of years so there is no room for indifference or apathy. When requesting their participation, be honest as you explain your hope that they be fully committed to the process. It is usually best to arrange a meeting with potential auxiliary members to discuss the process and your request face-to-face.

Generally, the sooner the person is involved in the transition process, the better. That way, valuable time is not spent reviewing past decisions and underlying rationales with the new team member. Also, seek input from auxiliary members as early as possible (ideally, when your child is reaching 14-16 years of age at the latest). To ensure their continued commitment, remember to take their needs into account when scheduling team meetings, to have realistic expectations for their involvement, and to frequently express your appreciation.

Remember to Be Honest and Communicate Openly

When working together as a transition team, it is essential that everyone be honest and communicate freely regarding their own perceptions, expectations, concerns, or restrictions. No one should agree to complete a task that is beyond their abilities or available time, even if pressured by the transition team. Define each task clearly so that everyone is aware of what is expected. It is often advantageous to use an "action plan" worksheet to delineate each task that needs to be done, who has been assigned to complete the task, and timelines for when the task should be completed.

If you feel that your child's transition plan has gone off course, say so and provide constructive suggestions to help the team get back on track. Do not misdirect your anger or frustration. For example, if a previously chosen work setting falls through because of changes in funding, do not blame it on the job trainer. As mentioned above, the transition process takes place over a number of years and can be quite emotionally taxing. Therefore, the more effectively and honestly you can support one another, the better.

Concluding Comments

Parents and guardians should begin the process of creating a transition team long before the student with autism graduates from high school. Many parents have reported that it can be such an overwhelming process that it is difficult to know where to start. Also, when children are young, parents are so busy working with the school and with their child to help him grow and develop that reallocating some of that time and energy to plan for something that seems vague and far off in the future seems unnecessary. However, this is a good time to remember the truth that it is easier to address something big in very small pieces.

Some families start the transition process by gathering a small group of trusted individuals (family members, teachers, friends, clergy—whoever is significant in the child's world) and sitting down to brainstorm a list of questions regarding transition that covers every possible area imaginable. This is not the time to talk about possible solutions, or what could happen, but just to focus on the questions. This can provide you with an initial blueprint of what you want to know. In fact, families have reported that the act of doing this actually helped them to begin identifying what they did and did not want to happen during the transition process. Having a concrete list of things to find out also helped to alleviate the anxiety of the unknown. It made the process seem increasingly manageable, and prepared them with many ideas and questions for the professionals who gathered at the table.

The Autism Society of America (ASA) states that the school system should provide the basis for transition planning. When the parents and school personnel effectively partner together to come up with the overall direction for the process and the services needed to move in that direction, a strong foundation is created for the many other transition team members who will eventually be involved in the transition process. Just such a collaborative, multilayered process is essential for a successful launching from high school for the young adult with autism.

4 | Early, Middle, and Later Phases of Transition

As stated in earlier chapters, the transition goals during a student's school age education must align with his or her life outcomes. In this chapter, we will examine the focus areas for educators, parents, and agencies during the early, middle and later phases of transition planning. With so many areas to address and skills to build, everything cannot be accomplished at one time. Therefore, we will explore which areas to concentrate on during which phases of transition. It is important to note that the later transition is started, the quicker a student will need to be moved through each transition phase.

All students benefit from best practices in teaching. Once your child has entered the transition period, it will be especially crucial to ensure that she is receiving instruction that enables her to make meaningful progress. Her instruction should be frequently monitored and examined by members of her IEP transition team. Many teams find it beneficial to analyze data weekly and discuss the analysis on a monthly basis. As soon as you begin considering transition planning, you should begin keeping a transition portfolio for your child or student.

Keeping a Transition Portfolio

There are a myriad of considerations and decisions to be made during the transition phase, and keeping a paper trail for each area will be extremely beneficial. Parents should take ownership of a portfolio for keeping any paperwork related to the areas of transition.

A good way to keep everything organized is to use an accordion folder or a binder with two-pocket folders labeled with each of the areas of transition: 1) postsecondary education, 2) employment, 3) living arrangements, 4) community involvement, 5) leisure activities, and 6) interagency linkages. Transition-related documents to have in your portfolio include:

- IEPs,
- results of assessments,
- applications for jobs and schools,
- resumes,
- emergency contact information,
- financial records,
- medical information, and
- other paperwork that relates to each area of transition.

Organizing these documents for easy access is important because this paperwork may be needed to support a change in services or a new service after your child leaves high school.

During your child's school years, the educators and agency members can help you create this portfolio. Ensure, however, that you have access to and copies of *all* paperwork related to transition. You and/or your child will be responsible for maintaining the portfolio after your child leaves high school.

Early Phases of Transition Planning

As stated in Chapter 2, IDEA requires that transition planning begin at age 16 and some state laws mandate a starting age of 14. The information in this chapter about the early phase of transition is meant to guide teams no matter when they begin to plan for moving a student from school to adult life. In an ideal IEP program, planning for life outcomes beyond school would begin as soon as the child enters elementary school. Unfortunately, most families are not ready to look that far ahead because they believe that would mean lowering expectations. That is not at all what it means! Targeting life outcomes can begin as early as kindergarten as long as we are looking at ways to teach a student to communicate, participate, solve problems, observe, read, and write.

Students with ASD become eligible for specially designed instruction for a wide variety of reasons. Often, however, it is because they demonstrate deficits in the areas of expressive and receptive commu-

A Word about Passions

Many students with autism spectrum disorders have one or more "passions"—activities or interests that they often choose to occupy themselves with and that they can be quite rigid about performing. For example, one student might want to frequently talk about trains and not notice other people's nonverbal cues that they are tired of hearing about the subject. Or, another student might like hair and constantly want to touch it. This is a socially unacceptable passion that needs to be redirected and replaced by a more acceptable behavior.

At your child's IEP meetings, it will be helpful to have a discussion about your child's passions, how they impede her independence, and perhaps how they can be used to help your child learn needed skills. The educators on your child's team might gather information about her passions through:

- reinforcement surveys (Reinforcers are highly preferred items for which a student will complete less desired tasks. Many commercial tools can be used to assess what items and activities are reinforcing to a student.)
- observation
- family interviews

It is critical for all members of the IEP team to work together to identify which passions are strengths and can foster education. For example, if the student has a passion for trains, can she be motivated to learn to write about trains or to do math problems involving trains? The team must also identify which passions may interfere with education and daily living. Those passions (behaviors) that are determined to interfere with the student's independence are best addressed by professionals with background in Applied Behavior Analysis (ABA) so that such behaviors can be extinguished and replaced in a systematic, efficient, and sustaining manner.

Early Phase of Transition — Levels of Independence		
Focus Area	**Questions to Think About**	**Who Can Help?**
Expressive Communication	■ Does the student understand the concept of communication? i.e., interaction with others helps me get needs and wants met. ■ Does the student have a method to independently communicate needs and wants? ■ Can others outside of the student's inner circle understand what he or she is trying to communicate? ■ How does the student's expressive communication affect participation in the general education curriculum? ■ How much support does the student need to use her communication method?	■ Speech and Language Therapist ■ Assistive Technology Professional
Receptive Communication	■ Does the student understand the concept of communication? i.e., interaction with others helps me respond to the needs and wants of others. ■ Does the student have a method to respond to others and to the environment? ■ Do others understand how to communicate with the student in a way that he or she understands? ■ How does the student's receptive communication affect participation in the general education curriculum? ■ How much support does the student need to understand what others are trying to communicate?	■ Speech and Language Therapist ■ Assistive Technology Professional

Social Interaction Skills	■ Does the student initiate appropriate interaction with adults? With peers? ■ Does she respond independently and appropriately when interacting with adults? ■ How does the student's ability to interact socially affect participation in the general education curriculum? ■ How much support does the student require to initiate and/or respond to others? ■ How do any challenging behaviors such as aggression, withdrawal, reaction to various stimuli affect her learning and functioning in the community?	■ Special Education Teacher ■ Speech and Language Therapist ■ Behavior Specialist ■ Occupational Therapist
Repetitive Behaviors and Interests	■ Does the student engage in actions or behaviors that interfere with her ability to independently navigate through the school day? ■ How much support does the student need to redirect any stereotyped (seemingly purposeless, repetitive) behaviors or passions? (See box.)	■ Special Education Teacher ■ Speech and Language Therapist ■ Behavior Specialist ■ Occupational Therapist
Activities of Daily Living	■ Is the student as independent in activities such as toileting, feeding, grooming, and hygiene as peers? ■ Can the student tell time, use the telephone, understand money and measuring concepts? ■ Can the student independently and safely navigate within the environ-ments that she encounters on a daily basis? ■ Does the student understand the concept of safety? Can she respond appropriately to emergencies? ■ How much support does the student need to complete activities of daily living?	■ Special Education Teacher ■ Speech and Language Therapist ■ Behavior Specialist ■ Occupational Therapist

nication, social interaction skills, and repetitive or rigid interests and activities. Since this is a spectrum disorder, the needs of students and the programming to address the needs will vary in scope and intensity for every student.

In early phases of transition, teams are encouraged *to begin where the student is.* That is, it is helpful to assess the *student's level of independence* in expressive and receptive communication, in social interaction skills, and in activities of daily living. It is also useful to understand how the student's rigid interests and passions might affect her education. Let's explore some questions that teams might consider during the early stage of transition.

Using the answers to the questions in each area, your child's IEP transition team can determine the appropriate programming to help increase her independence. For example, if a particular student currently uses a combination of a picture exchange method and signing to communicate with verbal prompting from adults, the team will want to consider what the next step towards independence is using these methods. If the team realizes that the student uses picture exchange with more independence than she uses sign, the team may request an assistive technology assessment to determine whether the student's relative strength in using pictures can be expanded through the use of technology. The goal would be to limit the student's dependence on adult prompts for communication.

Developing or increasing your child's independence should be the primary goal in the early stages of transition. Your IEP team should methodically develop specially designed instruction and related services with the next benchmark of faded supports in mind. The team should also consider your child's rate of learning and her need for repetition, maintenance, and generalization of skills through each stage of the learning process. Only then can your child's team begin to consider if the vision that they have for her is realistic.

Middle Phases of Transition Planning

Depending on the student's age, teams may need to move quickly to the middle phases of transition. They may spend only a year or two in the early phases if transition planning began at age 16, assuming the student will continue in school beyond age 18 or 19. If a team started transition planning when the student was in middle school even prior to the age mandated by laws, the middle phase of transition could begin between the ages of 14 and 16. Typically during the middle phase of transition planning, a student is either entering high school or has been there for a year or two.

During the middle phase of transition, you can begin to focus more specifically on life outcomes for your child. That is, what does the team want your child to know and be able to do once she leaves school? Life outcomes include living arrangements, employment or day-to-day activities, interaction in the community, and leisure activities. The IEP team will focus on the areas that the law requires for transition and begin to outline specifics for programming. There are many considerations that team members will want to think about prior to sitting down to draft the IEP.

The questions in this next chart will help the stakeholders who are supporting the student with ASD through the middle phase of the transition process.

Once these questions are answered, the IEP transition team can begin to further define a comprehensive transition plan for the student with ASD. In an ideal world, this phase of transition would begin when the student is 12 to 14 years old. Why? Because in the United States today, the supports for transition stop once a student leaves high school. Beyond high school, there are no IEP transition teams that are mandated to continue the road map for the student. Moreover, for those parents who are looking at supported living and work opportunities for their child with ASD, there are simply not enough supports out there to meet the demand. The support systems that are created during the school years are what families have to continue supporting the student after she leaves high school.

Considering Options for Post-Secondary Education

If your child with ASD is headed in this direction, the team will want to ensure that she is on the academic path to graduation that will support entrance into a college or technical program. You and your child should work with guidance counselors to explore programs and supports that are available for students with disabilities. Students who do not have disabilities generally begin this process a year or two before high school graduation. For your child, it will probably make sense

Middle Phase of Transition—Life Outcomes: Abilities and Interest

Focus Area	Questions to Think About	Who Can Help?
Postsecondary Education	■ Does the student with ASD have a level of independent expressive and receptive communication skills that will support postsecondary schooling? ■ Does the student have the academic ability to succeed in her desired course of study at a postsecondary institution? ■ Is the student able to live independently? (Consider social skills, daily living skills, problem solving skills, transportation skills) ■ Does the student have self-advocacy skills that will support her ability to have needs and wants met in the postsecondary setting? ■ What supports and services would be necessary for the student to participate in postsecondary education? (e.g., specific accommodations such as a notetaker, additional time for assignments or tests or use of a calculator available through Section 504)	■ Special Education Teachers ■ Guidance Counselors ■ School Psychologists ■ Behavior Specialists ■ Speech and Language Therapists ■ Assistive Technology Consultants ■ Family Members ■ College/Technical School Admissions Officers
Employment	■ Does the student with ASD have a level of independent expressive and receptive communication skills that will support competitive employment? Supported employment? ■ Does the student have the aptitude to acquire skills in her desired area of employment? (See Chapter 2) ■ Is the student able to use transportation to get to a job? ■ Is the student able to perform activities of daily living required at a specific job site? (Work with employment counselors or vocational rehabilitation agencies to assess this area.)	■ Special Education Teachers ■ Guidance Counselors ■ School Psychologists ■ Behavior Specialists ■ Speech and Language Therapists ■ Assistive Technology Consultants

	- Does the student have behaviors that could impede the quality or quantity of work? - Can the student independently and safely navigate within the environments that she encounters on a daily basis? - Does the student have self-advocacy skills that will support her ability to have needs and wants met in the employment setting? - What supports and services would be necessary for the student to participate in employment? (e.g., a job coach, visual schedules, etc.)	- Family Members - Vocational Rehabilitation Counselors - Employment Counselors - Job Coaches
Living Arrangements	- Does the student with ASD have a level of independent expressive and receptive communication skills that will support independent living? Supported living in a group home setting? Supported living in an alternate setting? - Has the student acquired skills in activities of daily living that support independent living? Supported living in a group home setting? Supported living in an alternate setting? - Does the student have behaviors that could impede living in a specific type of living arrangement? - Can the student independently and safely navigate within the environments that she encounters on a daily basis? - Does the student have self-advocacy skills that will support her ability to have needs and wants met in a specific setting? - What supports and services would be necessary for the student to participate in a given setting? (e.g., assistance with meal planning, completing household tasks, financial and money management, etc.)	- Special Education Teachers - School Psychologists - Behavior Specialists - Speech and Language Therapists - Assistive Technology Consultants - Social Workers - Family Members - Agencies that provide therapeutic support, mobile therapy or behavior support services in the community

(continued on next page)

(continued from previous page)

Community Involvement/ Leisure & Recreational Activities	▪ Does the student with ASD have passions and interests that can be linked to leisure and recreational activities? What community opportunities can the student with ASD explore for potential involvement? ▪ Can the student continue with these activities post-graduation? ▪ Can the student independently and safely navigate within the environments that she encounters on a daily basis? ▪ Does the student have self-advocacy skills that will support her ability to have needs and wants met in a specific setting? ▪ What supports and services would be necessary for the student to participate in a given setting? (e.g., transportation to the activity, assistance with personal care)	▪ Special Education Teachers ▪ Behavior Specialists ▪ Occupational Therapists ▪ Speech and Language Therapists ▪ Social Workers ▪ Family Members ▪ Agencies that provide therapeutic support, mobile therapy, or behavior support services in the community
Interagency Involvement	▪ Has the student and her family been involved with agencies such as the state or local Office for Developmental Disabilities? ▪ Does the student need assistance getting government benefits such as Medicaid? ▪ What roles should the educational and community agencies take to support the student's transition? (See Chapter 3.)	▪ Special Education Teacher ▪ Family Members ▪ Social Workers ▪ Agencies that provide therapeutic support, vocational support, or behavior support services in the community

to begin earlier. You will probably need extra time to find a school or program that will be a good fit.

Chapter 1 provides an overview of the types of postsecondary schools that may be appropriate for students with autism spectrum disorders. If you or your child are unsure which of these types of programs might be best for her, here are some steps you might take:

1. Read books or directories targeted to students with learning disabilities who are considering college (see Resource Guide at the back of the book).
2. Arrange a visit to a program you are considering.
3. Speak to students with disabilities and their families about their experiences in a particular school/program (the school may be able to help you find alumni/students to talk with).
4. Explore listservs or chatrooms on the Internet that focus on high functioning autism or Asperger's disorder where members talk about experiences related to postsecondary education.
5. During the last two years of school, explore a dual enrollment with a local college (if available) so that the student can explore options prior to graduation.

In addition to narrowing down what type of school or program your child might attend after high school, it will also be important to look into any testing that might be required as a prerequisite to attending the school.

- *Will your child be required to take the ACT or SAT to get into the college of her choice?* If so, you need to request testing accommodations well in advance of the test and be prepared to supply documentation proving that your child needs accommodations. If your child tends to do poorly on standardized tests but still has potential to succeed in college, you might want to research the schools that do not require SAT/ACT tests for admittance. See www.FairTest.org under "University Testing" for a list.

- *Will your child need to provide IQ or achievement test scores to get into a program or to receive accommodations under Section 504?* If so, how old can the scores be? Do you need to arrange for the high school to do particular evaluations of your child while she is still eligible for evaluations under IDEA? (Doing so can save you a great deal of money, as private evaluations can run into the thousands of dollars.)

Keeping in mind that a student with ASD can remain in public school until age 21 or until she receives a high school diploma, the stakeholders will want to begin looking into postsecondary options as early as the student's first year in high school. To be highly prepared for postsecondary education, some students with ASD require a couple of extra years to complete both the general education requirements and their specially designed program within the IEP.

Considering Options for Employment

Using the answers to the questions in the chart above, the team will want to focus on a specific type of employment that may be appropriate for your child—either right out of high school or after she completes postsecondary education or training. Sometimes, however, the answers point to a need for more information. More specialized assessments may be necessary to determine your child's present skill levels, as well as her aptitude for skill attainment. A Career Center, Office of Vocational Rehabilitation, or another rehabilitation service in your area may be a starting place for such an assessment. Bear in mind that there may be a waiting list to obtain an evaluation, so do not put this off too long.

The highly effective IEP transition team will work together to generate assessments appropriate for your child. For example, the team can begin assessing whether a student has the interest or skills to perform a particular job. Oftentimes, educators, occupational therapists, and job trainers can work together to research specific jobs and develop a task analysis of skills that are required to perform those skills. To do so, they will break down the skill into its component skills for easier teaching. For example, if a student is putting together a sample kit for a mouthwash product, the task analysis may include:

1. Fold one long end of the box to the center.
2. Bend the long end of the box so it stands up.
3. Fold the second long end of the box to the center.
4. Bend the second long end of the box so it stands up.

5. Fold one short side of the box on the perforated line.
6. Unfold from the perforated line.
7. Fold the two tabs on each side of the short end inward.
8. Fold the side into the center of the box on the fold line.
9. Bend the short side of the box so it stands up.
10. Fold the perforated line, keeping the tabs folded to the bottom of the box.
11. Insert the tabs into the slot on the side of the box.
12. Unfold the tabs on the outside of the box.
13. Repeat steps 5-11.
14. Place the mouthwash bottle in the box.
15. Place the coupon in the box.
16. Repeat step 12.
17. Tape the box.
18. Place the box in the large carton.

The student can then be evaluated on her ability and aptitude for that job.

Your child's IEP team should write goals and objectives that will lead to your child developing needed work skills. Subsequently, job-training experiences can be designed enabling your child to learn and practice work skills in competitive and/or supported employment.

The middle phase of transition is a time to try out different types of employment. Job experiences can be built into the your child's school day via the IEP. These experiences could be within the school setting or at a nearby community agency or business. Some students may find it beneficial to get part-time jobs if they are old enough to do so. The IEP team needs to determine what is best for each individual child based on the data provided by observations and assessments.

If the student still needs to work on prerequisite skills required for specific jobs, the teacher and job coach should work to design tasks that will build these skills. For example, if a student wants a clerical position but is a slow typist, time should be built into the school day for the student to improve this skill. If, however, this same student is unable, even with assistive technology, to perform the keyboarding skills required of a clerical support person, the educational team and vocational agency staff should use the data they glean from working with the student to discuss other employment options. Perhaps the student could answer phones and take messages or greet guests who enter an office.

As discussed in Chapter 1, competitive employment may not be a realistic option for some students with ASD. Working in a sheltered workshop may be a good alternative for some of these students. Similar to exploring options for postsecondary education, students and families can visit supported employment agencies. Additionally, many supported employment service organizations have personnel who will come to the school and perform assessments and explain programs that might be appropriate for students at individual IEP meetings. Dual enrollments in the supported work setting and in a high school program are options for IEP teams to consider for the student during the last two years of school.

Considering Options for Living Arrangements

There are various types of living arrangements to consider for your child with an ASD as she approaches her adult years. Each type of arrangement provides a different amount of support.

- **Home-based services**—Using this option, your adult child can continue to live in your home but receive services that free parents and other family members from some care giving responsibilities (and may teach the adult with ASD needed skills). These services are provided by trained staff in the family home. Support areas include personal care, medical appointments, and grocery shopping.
- **Supported living**—In this arrangement, the adult with an ASD lives in her own apartment or other residence. She receives individual supports in her own home based on her specific needs. Types of supports may include assistance with budgeting, meal planning, transportation, and medical appointments.
- **Life sharing**—In this type of arrangement, an individual is carefully matched with a family who provide a home, companionship, and needed supports for the adult with an ASD. The family members are trained to provide supports to the individual so that she can meet her needs and achieve life goals.
- **Community homes**—These homes are also known as group homes. This arrangement provides a home and staff who assist each person with personal, social, and physical activities for up to twenty-four hours a day.

Parents and guardians who have even the slightest notion that their child may require any type of assisted living as an adult should work with agency personnel to *get on the list*. Some areas are reporting as much as a ten-year waiting list for group home living. It is better to search out living arrangement options and complete applications that you may later determine are not necessary than it is to wait until closer to graduation time to begin your quest. With the new attention to ASD as the incidence rate is rising, advocacy groups are putting pressure on agencies and politicians to provide resources for families who are seeking housing options for the adult with ASD. Still, there are not enough resources to go around.

While researching available options, the team must begin to plan for increasing your child's independent living skills. During the middle phase of transition, it is important to consider:

- the activities of daily living addressed in the early phase of transition as well as any new grooming or hygiene skills connected with entering adolescence or adulthood;
- your child's ability to independently feed herself and to purchase and prepare food;
- your child's ability to manage finances and health care.

How Much Do You Do for Your Child?

To ensure that nothing is left to chance, this is a good time for you, the parent, to make a list of all that you do for your child with ASD during the day. Write down everything—from waking her in the morning to reminding her to brush her teeth—for a period of two weeks to a month. You don't want to forget making appointments for haircuts and the dentist! Then, use the list to determine what you do for your child out of habit that she may be capable of doing herself. These are skills that you can begin to give her more responsibility for completing.

Talk with your child to determine where to start and what would help her complete each task. Also, communicate with the school team to determine how your child could practice the skill at school, if appropriate. School personnel can also assist you with task analyses of skills if you are having trouble teaching them at home.

Considering Options for Community Involvement/ Leisure & Recreational Activities

During elementary school years, parents often strive to have their children with ASD included in typical community activities as much as possible. Birthday parties, classes in art, music, or gym, Boy Scouts or Girl Scouts, and summer camps are just a few opportunities their child may be involved in. Often, however, as the student with ASD ages, the social differences become more apparent and opportunities in the community for leisure and socialization become more difficult to find. Likewise, there may not be as many options for middle school students to engage in social activities at school because the classes that were considered *specials* in elementary school have become more academically challenging. Recess is no longer a part of the school day and even the lunch period is shortened and structured.

As your child grows older, you and her educators need to become creative in your efforts to create opportunities for socialization. Club periods, particularly if they relate to your child's passions, are an excellent starting point. Guidance counselors can also assist the IEP transition team in seeking out opportunities or creating special socialization groups for students to generalize their skills. Middle school is a critical time for all students who are trying to determine their respective identities. For the student with ASD, the difficulties are compounded.

When a student with ASD leaves the school setting, she may not be inclined to develop relationships or activities within the home or community. However, leisure and recreation is critical to everyone's good physical and mental health. Due to difficulties with communication and social awkwardness, people with ASD will need assistance in finding activities to pursue outside of school. Here are some suggestions parents can use to build social opportunities for their teenaged or young adult children:

- Ask teachers if they would be willing to develop peer programs in the school setting that carry over to the community. For example, teachers might create a game, dance, or craft club during a middle school club period that is open to students with and without disabilities. Friendships made within the club setting might carry over to after school times.

- Advertise for a volunteer companion for your child at your church or school. Try to find someone who shares at least some of your child's interests.
- If students at your high school must accumulate a certain number of volunteer hours to graduate, check whether students can satisfy that requirement by volunteering to provide companionship for your child, accompany her on community outings to the bowling alley, movies, etc.
- Consider advertising for and paying for companions for your child with ASD.
- Consider getting together with families of other students with ASD to plan social opportunities such as parties, swimming, trips to play miniature golf, bowl, etc.

Interagency Involvement

There is **a lot** to do to prepare a student with ASD for life after graduation. No one can be expected to single-handedly prepare the student. Agencies bring a unique perspective to the team because they can assist with bridging the gap between school-age supports and post-graduation supports. Agencies can be very helpful in assisting with living arrangements and employment opportunities, not to mention exploring respite care facilities. They can also help families obtain funding.

Later Phases of Transition Planning

As with the early and middle phases of transition, this phase may begin earlier for some students than for others. The latest time to move into this phase is during the last two to three years of a teenager's time in school. This means that if an IEP team got a later start on transition planning, the team may need to combine some of the aspects of the middle phase with this later phase of transition. If you are in this situation, don't panic! It is easy to combine the two phases. It just means more work in a shorter amount of time.

The goals during the later phase of transition should center on narrowing the focus of programming to make sure that your child gains the skills she needs to move seamlessly from high school to adult life. The IEP goals should be written to incorporate her needs related

Later Phase of Transition—Life Outcomes

Focus Area	Questions to Think About	Who Can Help?
Postsecondary Education	In addition to the tasks that the family of any graduating student would undertake during the final high school year: ■ Is the student academically prepared for the postsecondary program that he/she will attend? Does he/she have the prerequisite skills and courses necessary? ■ Has the student contacted the school to begin the process of setting up necessary supports and services? ■ Is there a plan for the student to spend time orienting to the campus and campus life? ■ If the student will be living away from home, have you worked out a system to be kept informed about academic or social problems he/she encounters?	■ Special Education Teachers ■ Guidance Counselors ■ School Psychologists ■ Behavior Specialists ■ Speech and Language Therapists ■ Assistive Technology Consultants ■ Family Members ■ College/Technical School Admissions Officers
Employment	■ Is the student spending a portion of the week in an appropriate employment setting? ■ Is the student able to use transportation to get to a job, as she will need to after graduation? ■ Is the student able to perform activities of daily living required at a specific job site consistently and with as much independence as possible? ■ Is the student using self-advocacy skills to have needs and wants met in the employment setting? ■ Is the student accessing supports and services that would be necessary for her to participate in employment?	■ Special Education Teachers ■ Guidance Counselors ■ School Psychologists ■ Behavior Specialists ■ Speech and Language Therapists ■ Assistive Technology Consultants ■ Family Members ■ Vocational Rehabilitation Counselors ■ Employment Counselors ■ Job Coaches

	Questions	People/Agencies
Living Arrangements	■ Is the student using skills that she would need to use in the type of setting where she is expected to live after graduation? ■ Have behaviors that could impede living in a specific type of living arrangement improved or have accommodations been put in place? (e.g., if a student has difficulty sharing items such as a TV or CD player, ensure that there are duplicate items in the student's room) ■ Is the student independently and safely navigating within the environments that she encounters on a daily basis? ■ Is the student demonstrating self-advocacy skills that enable her to have needs and wants met in a specific setting? ■ Is the student accessing supports and services that would be necessary for her to participate in a given setting?	■ Special Education Teachers ■ Behavior Specialists ■ Occupational Therapists ■ Speech and Language Therapists ■ Social Workers ■ Family Members ■ Agencies that provide therapeutic support, mobile therapy, or behavior support services in the community
Community Involvement/ Leisure & Recreational Activities	■ Is the student regularly participating in community activities related to her passions and interests? ■ Is the student independently and safely navigating within the environments that she encounters on a daily basis? ■ Is the student demonstrating self-advocacy skills needed to have her needs and wants met in a specific setting? ■ Is the student accessing supports and services that would be necessary for her to participate in a given setting?	■ Special Education Teachers ■ Family Members ■ Social Workers ■ Agencies that provide therapeutic support, mobile therapy, or behavior support services in the community
Interagency Involvement	■ Have partnerships with agencies that the student/family can continue to access after graduation been firmly established?	■ Agencies that provide therapeutic support, vocational support, or behavior support services in the community ■ Legal Services ■ Financial Planner

to postsecondary education and/or employment, living arrangements and activities of daily living, community involvement, and leisure activities. In the most seamless transition plan, your child's final year of high school would involve her spending a portion of the day at school and another portion of the day in the setting that she will participate in after leaving high school.

Easing Your Child into Adult Life

It is difficult for *anyone* to navigate multiple changes at one time. If a student with an autism spectrum disorder is presented with too many changes too quickly, she may develop anxiety issues or shut down and fail. This means that changes that will be made after leaving high school should be introduced one at a time. For example, your child should not be asked to move out of your home and start a job simultaneously. Also, students with ASD should be given as much time as they need in order to adjust to each change before presenting another.

It is critical to start moving from school to life outcomes during the last two years of school. For example, once the type of employment is determined, your child should spend at least a portion of the week in that setting performing the work tasks. As she gets closer to leaving high school, she should ideally be spending full weeks in the new setting while supports from the school are faded. This provides a seamless transition from school to work. Similarly, your family and agency personnel can work with your child to become more involved in community leisure activities during the last two years of school. Then, as the final semester approaches, you can begin to plan for summer activities outside of the school setting.

Sometimes it is difficult to create a seamless transition from school to work or postsecondary education. In those situations, the IEP team must develop a program that helps to simulate the post-school activities to the best of their ability, using whatever resources are available. For example, providing a student with community-based instruction opportunities is critical to help prepare her for the differences between high school and college. If a student is going to eat in a cafeteria at college, the student could go to different buildings (businesses, hospitals, schools, etc.) that have cafeterias to learn to order and pay for meals in a cafeteria setting.

Teams will need to "think outside the box" to create opportunities for the student to try out activities that will prepare her for life after school. For example, if a student is planning to move into an apartment or group home and has never had a roommate, she could go to a sleep-over camp to experience sharing a room with a stranger. The key aspect of using a similar experience is that the student will require a coach or instructor to help her understand how to apply the similar experience to the ultimate real experience. Otherwise, the literal-thinking person with ASD potentially will have a harder time adjusting to life after high school.

Staying Receptive to Change

Flexibility is the key to surviving each phase of transition. As you answer the questions and research additional information during each transition phase, you may discover that your child has more skills in an area than you thought and can aim for a higher-level position in a competitive employment setting. That discovery opens many doors that may have been closed in early transition phases and may lead to a decision that your child should remain in high school beyond 18. Likewise, you may discover that the expectations that you have for your child or that the child has for herself may not have been realistic. That too may lead you to decide that your child should remain in high school longer.

Remember, once your child leaves the public school system, she will no longer be eligible for transition services and supports under IDEA. Your child's eligibility for special education will stop when she: 1) graduates from high school with a diploma, or 2) reaches age 21. Before you and your child decide that she should leave the public school system, you should carefully balance the pros and cons:

If the goal is for your child to attend a postsecondary institution such as college, technical school, or a postsecondary program for students with disabilities:
- Does she need remedial work in any classes before she can be admitted to regular coursework at the college? What are the advantages of her doing the remedial work at the college vs. spending an extra year in high school doing the work?

■ Even if your child is academically qualified to go to college, would she benefit from more time in high school learning social skills or daily living skills that would help her succeed in a college environment?

■ Is your child unwilling to stay in high school after her classmates graduate?

■ Is it to your family's financial advantage for your child to remain in high school an extra year or two? (e.g., more time to save money for college tuition; issues related to eligibility for government benefits)

If the goal is for your child to begin a job immediately after leaving high school:

■ Does your child have the social, motor, communication, transportation, or other skills needed to succeed in the type of job she prefers? Could she continue to develop these through therapies, coaching, etc. at school if she remained in high school past age 18?

■ Does your child have the reading and math skills needed to live as independently as possible in the community?

■ Is your child unwilling to stay in high school after her classmates graduate?

■ Are there financial considerations related to her leaving school or getting a job? For example, if your child is no longer a full-time student but is not considered disabled enough to receive Medicaid, she could lose health insurance coverage when she leaves school (assuming your health insurance policy only covers dependents who are full-time students).

If you have used the recommendations in Chapters 3 and 4, the obstacles to your child's dream and goals will have been discovered and addressed earlier in the process. Then, you have an entire support system in the IEP team to help you and your child overcome each stumbling block. It is also important to remember that even parents of students who do not have disabilities are going through some of the same things that you are. Their children may be initially focused on college, but then during senior year decide that they do not want to go. Perhaps a student has been attending a technical school during high school and during the job experience decides this isn't what she thought it would be. It's okay if plans for your child change too. Step back, take a breath, and reach out to others for support.

If your child has not achieved a diploma and is under age 21, you can continue to work with her transition team and devise a new transition plan. If she is approaching age 21 or is on track to get a diploma, the educational team is limited in the help they can offer post-graduation. However, they would still likely point you in a direction that can provide assistance. After all, they want your child to succeed just as much as you do.

Not only should IEP transition teams be prepared for changes in the student but also for changes in the laws and systems. For example, if your child is moving toward postsecondary education and your school district requires students to pass high stakes tests in order to graduate, the team must be aware of such requirements. Under the NCLB Act, accountability requirements for districts and students are changing yearly. It is critical that IEP transition teams be prepared to revise programs so that students can meet the specified criteria. Revisions that team members should be prepared to make to your child's IEP include:

- revising goals and objectives,
- adding related services such as assistive technology or behavior supports if they are not already included,
- providing tutoring,
- pre-teaching skills that will be needed, or
- adding accommodations or modifications to the IEP.

Additionally, the team needs to pay attention to the postsecondary program your child has selected and make adjustments to your child's instructional program if entrance requirements change or the program ceases to be available.

5 | Involving Your Child with an ASD in the Transition Process

One of the most difficult tasks during transition is deciding just how much involvement should be expected from the student with an autism spectrum disorder. Because the autism spectrum includes a wide range of skills, abilities, cognitive levels, and communication proficiency, there is no one-size-fits-all formula for determining how much to involve each individual. One common mistake, however, is for parents and professionals to underestimate the degree to which the student can actively participate. To assure that your child's interests are fully covered, it is imperative to involve him as much as possible. This will increase the overall success of the transition process because your child will feel as if he is an active participant and therefore be more apt to cooperate in the development and implementation of the transition plan.

There are certain fundamental considerations to keep in the forefront when considering involvement of your child with an ASD. Of course, one of the first questions that needs to be asked is, "How well can he truly understand the transition process?" If he has a dual diagnosis of an ASD and an intellectual disability (mental retardation), his cognitive limitations will inevitably influence his ability to fully understand the overall process, as well as to follow along during discussions regarding possible vocational or living arrangements. At the same time, never assume that an individual with an ASD cannot participate at all if he has intellectual deficits. Rather, transition team members need to be creative in thinking of ways to allow choice making and help the individual understand discussions and decisions. For example, for a nonverbal student who has an intellectual disability, you can provide pictures of potential work settings and ask him to point to a preferred job.

Specific Issues to Consider When Involving a Student with an ASD

Literal Thinking

Inherent to developing a transition plan is the need to think hypothetically. That is, you need to be able to *imagine* different jobs or living situations as well as *imagine* how you would respond to them. Unfortunately, one of the more consistent characteristics of individuals with autism spectrum disorders, even for those with average to above average intelligence, is that they tend to think very literally. Therefore, it can be incredibly difficult for young people with ASDs to imagine themselves in various employment or living situations.

This tendency toward thinking concretely can drastically hinder the transition process if the team relies primarily upon merely *describing* vocational and living options during planning. Individuals with ASDs usually need to *see* and *experience* potential work and living situations personally before they can provide genuine feedback regarding their preferences. Although the most common way of providing this experience is personal exposure, sometimes watching a videotape or looking at pictures of the prospective work or living situation can be sufficient. However, as a general rule, personal experience is usually your best route in order to assure your child's full comprehension.

A related recommendation is to carefully choose your wording during your interactions with the person with an ASD. Try to void idioms or unclear statements, as these will only promote confusion. One student we know refused to work in a particular setting because he heard that a colleague at the site was a prankster who liked to "pull people's legs"; our student had an image of this person doing exactly that and wanted no part of it! It is best to rely upon clear, concrete terms rather than merely providing additional descriptions to try to help the student understand your point. As one student with

Asperger's disorder noted, "Neurotypical people try to *expand* communication, while people on the autism spectrum just try to decrease *miscommunication*." Using fewer words that are clear and to the point is your best bet.

Remember the "Triad of Symptoms"

As you may recall, there are three primary clusters of behaviors that are present in individuals with autism spectrum disorders. These are:

1. qualitative impairments in social skills,
2. qualitative impairments in communication, and
3. the presence of ritualistic and repetitive behaviors or interests.

When making transition decisions regarding a student with an ASD, there are certain general axioms that tend to ring true given these three areas of concern. These axioms, discussed below, include:

1. Do not overtax social skills.
2. Consider passions and preoccupations.
3. Respect the need for routine and predictability.
4. Do not overtax communication skills.

Do Not Overtax Social Skills

Focus on vocational and living situations that do not demand excessive social interactions or the ability to interpret interpersonal nuances. Most individuals with ASDs find it exceedingly difficult to perform successfully in social situations. Therefore, they are more comfortable in less socially-oriented job or living situations. Of course, although this is usually the case, this statement is an overgeneralization to some extent because some individuals on the autism spectrum enjoy social interactions. Directly observe the individual's social skills and his interest in social activities, and interview people who know him well to help determine how socially demanding the chosen work or living situation should be.

Consider Passions and Preoccupations

Try to incorporate your child's passions and preoccupations when making transition decisions. It is often helpful to take advantage of any specific areas of interest (especially a passion) and try to customize your child's employment or living situation accordingly while still accommodating for his overall skill level. For example, a student may be especially interested in trains and want to be an engineer, but does not have the cognitive skills for this to be a realistic goal. If so, you could explore other vocations that are linked to trains but are more within the individual's skill set. In the same vein, if a student is especially interested in history, he may be more amenable to moving into a group home if you point out that it is near the local museum.

If potential "spin-off" jobs are not readily apparent to you, sit down with someone in the community who has a job within your child's area of interest and ask him or her to describe related jobs that may be within your child's abilities. Although individuals on the autism spectrum usually maintain the same passions over the years, it is a good idea to keep a running list of interests/passions that develop and to share this information with relevant transition team members.

Respect the Need for Routine and Predictability

Focus on vocational and living situations that are generally routinized and predictable. People with ASDs are usually more content when each day at work and home is relatively consistent with a minimum of surprises. Clear structure and predictable schedules tend to be appealing and lead to a greater degree of success.

As a general rule, you will want to avoid jobs that demand quick changes in routine or multitasking. Again, it might make sense to sit down with someone in the community who has the job that is being considered and ask them to describe a typical day. Or, you might ask to actually observe the person in the work setting. If the job involves many transitions and unexpected surprises, this would probably not be an ideal job for most people on the autism spectrum.

Do Not Overtax Communication Skills

Consider vocations and living situations that do not require ongoing or sophisticated communication. A work setting that requires a lot of talking during the day will be highly taxing to most individuals with an autism spectrum disorder. Quiet work that the individual can focus upon without any demands for language is usually a better fit. Similarly, a living arrangement where the other housemates are generally quiet and do not feel the need for ongoing conversation will probably be less anxiety-provoking as compared to a setting where a lot of dialogue is expected.

Strategies to Increase Student Involvement

Mentors

Many highly successful adults with an ASD cite the support of a mentor as one of the major reasons for their success. Once a potential employment situation is chosen, the transition team should try to identify a mentor in the field who is willing to work with the individual with an ASD.

Mentors are usually found through networking and it can take some time before a viable mentor is identified. More often than not, the mentor has some vested interest either in the given student with an ASD and/or in individuals with developmental differences in general. (For example, they may have a family member with a disability.) Personality characteristics that are essential in a mentor include patience, sensitivity, and understanding of the idiosyncrasies of autism spectrum disorders.

If your child will be working with a mentor, it is beneficial for people who know him to meet with the mentor ahead of time to provide relevant information. For example, you, another family member, or a teacher who knows your child well could let the mentor know about your child's communication style and potential behavioral quirks.

The time and commitment a mentor is willing to put in can vary. One might agree to see your child on a weekly basis within the work setting, while another might be willing to meet periodically with your child to discuss the transition process and answer any questions about the given vocation. Some mentors become part of the IEP transition team as an auxiliary member. (See Chapter 3.)

On occasion, the mentor can be another person with an ASD who is sufficiently adept to serve as an effective role model. This type of mentoring relationship can be especially advantageous in helping a student understand the transition process. At times, we have set up email contacts between students in the transition process and adults on the autism spectrum who are working successfully in a distant location. Although this type of long-distance relationship has its limitations, it can also be a viable means of providing support from "someone who knows" without the added social pressure of face-to-face contact.

The transition team needs to provide mentors with sufficient information and training in order to assure that they can be as effective as possible. The mentor should be provided guidance in terms of what type of language and supports would be most useful when guiding the individual with an ASD. The mentor should also be aware of the level of commitment expected ahead of time so that he will not later feel imposed upon or end his relationship as a mentor before the transition process is complete.

Provide Guided Choices

When helping a student with an ASD to begin choosing a vocation or living situation, it is usually better to provide guided choices rather than asking open-ended questions. Individuals with ASDs usually find questions such as "What kind of job do you want?" or "Where would you like to live?" to be highly confusing, most likely due to their difficulties imagining as well as their lack of exposure to options. Therefore, it makes sense to generate a list of potential jobs or living situations and then present them to your child in groups of two to four possibilities so that he is not overwhelmed.

Every once in a while, a student with an ASD is able to actually generate his own list of potential careers and it is important for everyone on the transition team to take these options as seriously as possible. (See the section on "Involving Students with Asperger's Disorder or High Functioning Autism," below.)

Visual Supports to Assure Comprehension and Promote Success

Most people with ASDs take information in more effectively via visual input than through their other senses. As a result, various techniques have been developed to teach individuals with ASDs with the help of "visual supports." At the very least, it is often beneficial to supplement verbal descriptions with pictures or gestures in order to increase the student's understanding during the transition process. However, there are other, more refined, methods of providing information via visual supports that you can consider incorporating into the transition process. These include:

- Social Stories,
- Comic Strip Conversations,

- Written schedules,
- Power Cards, and
- Video modeling.

Social Stories

As created and refined by Carol Gray, Social Stories™ involve writing an individualized storybook from the perspective of the person with an autism spectrum disorder. These stories provide information in written and/or icon form to help the individual understand the social expectations of a given situation and the effect of his own behavior on others. They can also address the person's specific fears or idiosyncrasies. During the transition process, it can be helpful to write Social Stories about potential vocational or living situations.

Gray recommends that Social Stories include four types of sentences:

1. **Descriptive Sentences.** Descriptive sentences describe the "who, what, where, and when" factors of a given situation. Gray emphasizes that the majority of the sentences in a Social Story should be descriptive in nature in order to help the person with an ASD comprehend as much as possible. These sentences should describe the situation truthfully and objectively and set the stage for the Social Story.

   When you write descriptive sentences, use qualified words such as "sometimes" and "usually" rather than absolutes such as "always" or "never," so that the individual with an ASD does not decide that the entire Social Story is incorrect if the one absolute statement proves untrue one day. Examples of descriptive sentences within a Social Story addressing transition could include:

   - *One of my future housemates, John, sometimes yelled really loudly when I visited the group home.*
   - *My supervisor at work will occasionally have to correct my work.*
   - *When I visit a new workplace, I usually don't know all the rules at first, like what time we eat lunch.*

2. **Perspective Sentences.** Perspective sentences point out other people's internal states, thoughts, beliefs, opinions, motivation, etc., within the social situation. Most

individuals with ASDs have great difficulty taking other people's perspectives, so perspective sentences help them to better understand how their actions affect others and how others may be feeling. Examples of perspective sentences within a Social Story regarding transition could include:

- *I guess John is feeling pretty mad when he starts to yell.*
- *My supervisor is only trying to help me when she corrects my work.*
- *Other people might not know how important it is for me to know what time lunch break is scheduled.*

3. **Directive Sentences.** Directive sentences provide specific responses that the person with an ASD can consider using within the social situation. Directive sentences should include phrases such as "I will try to…" and "One thing I could do is…" rather than absolutes such as, "I will…." This decreases the amount of pressure placed upon the individual and makes the transition more of a choice. A common mistake for parents and staff is to include too many directive sentences because they are focusing more on what they want the student to *do* rather than on teaching him to better understand the social situation. Instead, a Social Story should have many more descriptive than directive sentences. Examples of directive sentences in a Social Story related to transition could include:

- *I could think about leaving the room and go to a quiet place when John starts to yell.*
- *I can try to listen carefully to my supervisor so that I don't make the same mistake again.*
- *I can choose someone at the new workplace who looks nice and ask them to tell me when they eat lunch.*

4. **Affirmative Sentences.** Affirmative sentences make general statements regarding life or provide overall encouragement to the reader. Affirmative sentences may exaggerate or enhance the meaning of other statements within the Social Story, or express a commonly accepted cultural norm. Some affirmative sentences serve to reas-

sure the individual with an ASD or validate his feelings.
Examples of affirmative sentences within a Social Story
about transition might include:

- *It will feel great if I can stay calm when John is yelling.*
- *Most people at work get corrected every once in a while.*
- *Learning the rules and schedule of a new job is a
  good thing to do.*

Using Social Stories can be a viable means to help your child with
an ASD to better understand the relevant factors surrounding a work or
living situation and facilitate a smoother transition. For a more comprehensive review of this technique, visit Carol Gray's website, thegraycenter.
org, or look at the various written and videotaped training materials
produced by Ms. Gray and others in the field.

Sample Social Story

What does a completed Social Story look like? Let's say that
an adolescent with an ASD is set to start a new job within a
few days. A Social Story for him might look something like this:

On Monday, I'm scheduled to start my new job at the grocery store.
I am supposed to help the other workers put cans of food on the
shelves and maybe bag the groceries at the checkout too.

It's a new job and sometimes new things can be confusing
and make me nervous. I might not know the schedule or how to
do the job. That's okay. Most people are at least a little confused
and nervous on the first day of a new job. I can try to stay calm
by taking deep breaths and focusing on my job. When I visited the
grocery store during my interview, the people seemed pretty nice
and said they would be willing to help me. So, if I feel confused I
can just ask someone for help.

My mom will be really happy if I follow my boss's instructions and talk nicely when I'm at the new job. My new coworkers
might like it when I do my job well. It will probably get easier and
easier each day that I go to my job. If I stay calm and do my job,
I'll be proud of myself and be able to buy some CDs when I get
my first paycheck!

Comic Strip Conversations

Another technique developed and promoted by Carol Gray is "Comic Strip Conversations." Comic Strip Conversations are similar to Social Stories, but rely upon simple sketches as the primary means of providing information to the individual with an ASD. Stick-figure drawings with prescribed symbols help the individual with an ASD understand what other people may be thinking within a given social context and also provide alternative behaviors the student can use during similar situations in the future. Color coding may be used to help the student with autism understand the other person's feelings.

For students who are transitioning, Comic Strip Conversations could be written about many issues. For example, they might cover:

- how a job coach may react if the student refuses to cooperate versus when he is cooperative,
- how parents may be feeling about their son or daughter with an ASD growing up,
- what a prospective employer may be thinking during a job interview,
- others' reactions when the individual with an ASD begins to make loud noises at a work place versus when the person works quietly, or
- how parents and potential housemates may be feeling during an initial visit to a supervised apartment setting.

Written Schedules

Another visual support that is often used with students with autism spectrum disorders is a written schedule. Written schedules can consist of custom-made schedules involving pictures or words or commercially available calendars or appointment books. They may be used to help the student understand the sequence of events involved in the transition process, as well as mini-steps within each step of transition. For example, your child's transition team can develop a calendar that notes the dates of important transition events such as upcoming job interviews, visits to potential work settings, and visits to supervised living arrangements.

Power Cards

Power Cards are another visual strategy that can help the transition process go more smoothly for students with autism spectrum disorders who are overly focused on certain objects, celebrities, fictional characters, etc. The Power Card concept was developed by Elisa Gagnon to increase motivation when teaching people with ASD to respond appropriately, especially during social situations.

To use this strategy, the transition team would first identify the student's particular passion (such as a favorite celebrity or topic). They would then write up a one-page story incorporating the passion and focusing on the appropriate behavior.

If a student with an ASD can associate the desired appropriate behaviors with his passion, he will sometimes be more motivated to use those behaviors. For instance, one student was especially preoccupied with weather and the local weatherman. We wrote a one-page story about the weatherman's first job interview, describing how he had used appropriate social skills such as initiating and maintaining eye contact, smiling, and staying on topic. We then summarized the most important points of the story on a 3 x 5 "Power Card." This card included a picture of the weatherman, as well as bullets describing the major behaviors that we wanted the student to remember during his own job interview. The student used it as a cue card during his own job interview and performed quite well, due to the link between his favorite celebrity and the expected behaviors.

Video Modeling

One of the more recent innovations that can be used to promote a smooth transition is video modeling. This strategy involves making a short film that focuses on the specific aspects of a given task or social situation that you want to emphasize to an individual with an ASD. For example, you can make a videotape of someone taking turns during a conversation. Or, if you are teaching an individual with an ASD to perform a specific vocational task, you can videotape another person performing the task and zoom in on aspects of the task that are especially important for the student to remember. Using the zoom lens during filming can be especially advantageous because it prompts the student to pay attention to the most relevant aspects of the situation.

For the best results and to increase the student's willingness to watch the tape, make sure that the actor(s) in the videotape are especially appealing to the student with ASD (e.g., a favorite paraprofessional or the student's sibling). If your student or child enjoys watching *himself* on tape, you can create a videotape that depicts him performing the desired task. (This is known as video self-modeling.) For example, we worked with one student who took 30 minutes to get through his morning routine (e.g., hang up his coat, put away his homework, etc.) even though each step was well within his abilities. To create the videotape, one staff member did the videotaping as another staff prompted the student with gestures from behind the camera to go through the morning routine at a more reasonable pace. The student then watched the videotape both at home and in school and was soon completing his morning routine in 5 minutes or less.

After making the videotape, have the student watch the tape a few times. As the student watches, do *not* make any comments about what is being viewed, but merely redirect the student's attention to the tape if he becomes distracted. After the student has watched the tape several times, make a general comment such as, "Your turn." Immediately role play the given social situation with the student, or take the student to a setting where he can use the positive behaviors observed in the tape. If you are teaching a vocational or academic task, instruct the student to watch the task and then provide the relevant instructional materials while saying, "Your turn." We have found video modeling to be an effective means of providing essential information to students with ASDs in a purely visual format.

Responding to the Emotional Aspects of Transition

Transition can be a difficult time for many students who are nearing graduation from high school, and students on the autism spectrum are no different than their typically developing peers in this regard. As the final days of transition approach, your child with an ASD may feel anxious, confused, resistant to the idea of change, or disappointed that his hopes for the future turned out to be unrealistic. If an older sibling has already left home to go off on his own, your child with an ASD may assume that he must follow exactly the same path (e.g., college) and consequently feel undue anxiety.

Starting the transition phase early in adolescence assures that your child will have the opportunity to be gradually exposed to the idea of leaving school and entering adulthood. This shaping process will make it more likely that he will have a clear picture of what is expected during transition. It is also important to continue to revisit transitional themes to remind your child what people do when they "grow up." For example, allow him to frequently watch a videotape of his prospective workplace, revisit a future group home, or visit older, adult siblings at their workplaces or homes. Do not assume that one exposure to these new situations is sufficient. In fact, assume that your child will need repeated exposure in order to fully grasp the idea of transition.

Helping Your Child Articulate His Feelings

Your child, like any other student who is approaching a new chapter in his life, needs to be able to discuss his feelings and concerns about transitioning out of high school. However, even the most adept students with ASDs often have trouble identifying and expressing their own emotions. Remember that students on the autism spectrum often find abstract concepts such as feelings to be incomprehensible. Therefore, your child may benefit from having specific IEP goals which focus on identification and expression of emotions as early as possible in his educational experience. This skill can be taught a variety of ways including via Social Stories™, software programs, role playing, social skills groups, and the like. Some students have learned to identify their own emotions using visual cues such as "emotional thermometers," periodically recording their emotional state on a pictured thermometer which shows various levels of emotional states.

Once your child has learned to accurately express emotions, it is important to touch base with him every so often to assess his feelings regarding upcoming experiences within the transition process. At times parents need to be highly sensitive to behavioral changes that may reflect their child's emotions as transition steps take place. For example, your child may begin to demonstrate challenging behaviors while out on a work crew with the job coach, or make perseverative statements about a seemingly minor aspect of his day. Ask your child directly about these concerns and encourage him to communicate within whatever mode he is most comfortable. For example, one high school senior we know writes daily journal entries in which he expresses emotions that he has never been able to communicate verbally.

As is true for most adolescents in the general population, this transition period may be a time of heightened anxiety and/or depression. If your child appears overly depressed or anxious, consider consulting a psychologist or psychiatrist for advice.

Helping Your Child Cope with Change

Even typically developing students often have trouble coping with the changes involved in leaving high school. For students on the autism spectrum, just coping with the mere *idea* of change can be problematic. One characteristic of students on the autism spectrum is a tendency towards rigidity of thought and daily routine. Therefore, it is often necessary to teach these students to be more flexible and open to change.

One technique that can be helpful for parents who expect their children to have difficulties with the changes that transition will bring is "cognitive restructuring." This is a therapeutic method that can be highly effective when teaching students to change the way they think. For example, you can give your child cue cards that list adaptive, flexible thoughts such as, "Change is okay"; "Life is full of surprises"; and "Most people graduate from high school when they become an adult." If your child reads these cue cards frequently, the thoughts become ingrained in his cognitive processes. This, in turn, can help him become more open to the changes that come with transition. An especially useful resource in regards to using cognitive restructuring to teach individuals on the autism spectrum how to express emotions is Tony Attwood's *Exploring Feelings* series.

When Making Choices is Difficult

It is often difficult for students on the spectrum to communicate their choices. Some students are completely nonverbal, while even individuals who can speak in full sentences may still have difficulty making the simplest of choices. The IEP transition team must consequently be especially careful not to make choices *for* your child with an ASD. The team members need to consistently involve him in the decision-making process at all stages of the transition plan development to the highest degree to which he can participate. Given this goal, it is also important to teach your child to advocate for himself. For example, he needs to recognize that it is acceptable to disagree with the IEP team's ideas during transition and understand how to do so appropriately.

If a student is completely nonverbal or minimally able to communicate via speech, the transition team can prompt him to use other modes of communication such as signing, the Picture Exchange Communication System (PECS), or gestures to convey his wishes. Providing him with guided choices rather than open-ended ones can increase his comprehension and ability to respond. For example, ask, "Do you like working at McDonald's or Pizza Hut?" while showing him pictures of each option, rather than asking, "Where do you like to work the best?"

If your child or student is overwhelmed by even two choices, you may need to resort to yes/no questions to assess his preferences. If all else fails, you may need to interpret the student's body language, facial expressions, and willingness to participate in activities in order to determine his preferences for potential work or living settings.

Involving Students with Asperger's Disorder or High Functioning Autism

For the most part, the strategies noted throughout this chapter can be implemented when helping a student with high functioning autism (HFA) or Asperger's disorder to transition to adulthood. Remember, just because a student has exceptional academic abilities does not mean that he will not need the various supports outlined in this book. At the same time, one of the fundamental themes to keep in mind when working with higher functioning students with ASDs is to *promote independence*. It is vital that the IEP team consistently convey that they have confidence in the student's ability to transition successfully and independently.

In this vein, all team members, including parents, must allow the student as much independence as possible so that he can "own" the transition process. Whenever possible, permit the student with an ASD to lead the discussion during meetings, generate ideas, and weigh his options. Assign him or have him choose specific tasks as part of the transition process and follow up on his progress. For example, have him read through classified ads, set up meetings with potential housemates, or contact the colleges he is interested in attending for information on the application process. If he has difficulties organizing his time or prioritizing tasks, help him set a schedule and deadlines for accomplishing his tasks. Also, if he needs to use social skills that are difficult for him, such as calling a stranger on the phone, consider using a Social Story or other visual support to help him.

What does a parent do when their transitioning child identifies a goal that is clearly unrealistic? Just like all parents, you may be hesitant to burst your child's dreams with hard reality. However, it is also important for the IEP team as a whole (including the parents) to provide direct and concrete experiences for the adolescent so that he can make a realistic appraisal of his options. Do so in a diplomatic, yet honest manner by emphasizing your child's skills while noting tendencies which may make it difficult for the career to be achieved.

The most effective route is often to find a career goal which is *within the same genre* as the unrealistic job so that the individual on the autism spectrum can continue to be motivated. For example, if he is interested in becoming a doctor, perhaps he can explore careers as a medical lab technician, a medical transcriptionist, or a medical coding specialist in a position that requires fewer demands on his social skills. Or if he has his heart set on being a writer, perhaps he could look into employment as a librarian, indexer, or proofreader so he can work with books but also earn a living wage.

If two potential routes are equally viable, always follow the path preferred by the student with an ASD. The fundamental rule to keep in mind then is to convey respect at all times so that the student's confidence is enhanced.

Concluding Comments

One of the major axioms when involving students with autism spectrum disorders in the transition process is to "think outside the box"; in fact, throw out the box altogether! The transition team needs to be highly creative and individualized as they develop strategies for helping the student understand the many options available to him after high school. For the greatest chances of success, make sure that the student is as fully involved in the transition process as possible, regardless of his "functioning level."

6 | Beyond School

While the school years are regulated by IDEA, and students and families have significant rights and entitlements, the landscape changes dramatically once a student graduates. There is no federal mandate governing adult services for adults with autism, and matters are complicated by procedures for determining eligibility that vary greatly across the different agencies. Moreover, funding and eligibility determinations begin at the state level and then flow down through each level of government, so supports and services vary greatly from state to state and locale to locale. Additionally, there is little predictability from year to year as budgets determined by current administrations and priorities of the voters change according to the many other needs of each county. This post-school scenario accentuates the need for parents and IEP teams to be very strategic in planning during the school years.

Locating Supports and Services in Your Community

Supports and services beyond school for people with autism spectrum disorders are in the formative years. Some of the supports that may be available to your adult child include:

- Natural supports
  - ❑ Relatives and friends
  - ❑ Coworkers

❏ Neighbors
❏ Financial and legal advisors
■ Community supports
  ❏ Recreation centers
  ❏ Membership organizations
  ❏ Volunteer agencies
  ❏ Transportation services
  ❏ Job training services
  ❏ Advocacy organizations
  ❏ Religious organizations
  ❏ Senior services
  ❏ Adult education services

Other supports may be available through county offices of Mental Health/Mental Retardation (MH/MR) or the Office of Developmental Disabilities (names for these agencies vary from community to community). Services available from the MH/MR/ODD office may include:

■ locating services to assist adults with disabilities in the home (with daily care, housekeeping, budgeting, shopping, etc.)
■ helping adults to find and retain employment,
■ assisting with locating groups or organized leisure activities, or
■ helping individuals find a place to live.

Funding for such services often comes from federal, state, and local governments. Services vary by state; but often each state has services related to the following categories:

■ Mental retardation/developmental disabilities
■ Mental health
■ Vocational rehabilitation
■ Health and human services
■ Aging

Unfortunately, once your child leaves high school, you will no longer have a service coordinator, case manager, or other professional whose job is to help you locate and coordinate the resources and supports your child needs. Instead, you will likely need to function as your child's case manager, seeking out the services that she needs, figuring out sources of funding, determining how to fill in gaps in services, etc.

Some of the best ways to get an overview of the adult services available in your community are:
1. Networking with other parents in your community;
2. Contacting local organizations to find out about opportunities in your community;
3. Contacting national organizations to find out about federal programs that your child may benefit from.

Other Parents: Often other parents whose adult children are a few years older than yours can be the best source of practical information about finding and accessing services in your community. If your child has not graduated from high school yet, make an effort to meet other parents of students with disabilities at PTA meetings, back-to-school nights, or other school-sponsored functions. Ask your child's teachers if they can connect you with a few parents whose challenges are similar to your child's (if they are not allowed to give you the contact information for other parents, ask if they will forward an email or note from you to them.)

If your child has already left high school, there are many ways to find parents of other young adults within your community. Search the Internet for listservs and bulletin boards for families of children with ASD. For example, if you go to the home page for Yahoo! Groups (www.yahoogroups.com) and type in "autism" and the name of your state in the search box, you will likely be able to locate at least a couple of support groups in your general area. There may also be support groups for parents of children with ASD or developmental disabilities in your community that have meetings you could attend. Local and online support groups are forming every day in order to focus on post-graduation. Such resources should be tapped to brainstorm ideas and to benefit from the experiences of others who may have encountered similar experiences.

Local Organizations: If there is a county chapter of the ARC, United Disability Services, Easter Seals, or any other organization that serves a broad spectrum of people with disabilities, that may be an excellent place to start your search for local resources. Often these types of organizations will have someone on staff who is knowledgeable about adult services in your area. They may also sponsor workshops or talks about accessing adult services, guardianship, qualifying for state or federal assistance programs, etc. Also, local medical groups and hospitals are sponsoring more workshops and supports for parents of children with disabilities. Examine newsletters and newspaper inserts for such activities.

National Organizations: National organizations such as the Autism Society of America or Autism Speaks.org can be a good source of information about nationwide programs that can benefit your adult child. For example, they may be able to provide information about qualifying for federal benefits such as Section 8 housing assistance or Medicaid benefits. If you attend these conferences, you will probably find at least some workshops that are devoted to adult issues.

Find Support for Yourself

Helping your child make the transition to adult life will likely be one of the most difficult experiences of your life. After all, for the last 18 to 21 years, this child has likely been at the center of many of your decisions, activities, and relationships. How are you supposed to turn some or all of these responsibilities over to your young adult child or someone else?

Remember, transition is a journey and will take time. The best way that you can support your child is to have supports for yourself as well. As you are pursuing some of the above avenues in searching out supports for your child, be sure to find out what supports they can offer you too.

- If you are networking online or in person in an attempt to locate services for your child, also try to make a personal connection with other parents who are in the same boat. Ideally, you can help each other problem solve and can bounce feelings and ideas off one another.
- If you attend local or national conferences, attend some workshops that are devoted to parental coping, marital stress, or the like.
- If your child is going away to college or another type of post-secondary program, check to see if the school offers lectures or other supports to help parents deal with "letting go."
- If you are truly feeling depressed or anxious about some aspect of the transition process, speak to your doctor

about it. There are many medical and psychological interventions that may help.

■ If you just want to start with someone to talk to about the
grieving process of your child not needing to be as dependent on you, consider contacting your spiritual advisor or
leaders within your place of worship.

It is natural to find some aspects of *letting go* to be very difficult,
even for parents of children with no diagnosed special needs. But, it
is a necessary part of parenthood. You can do it!

Practical Realities Post-Graduation

It is important to structure the changes that your child will need
to adapt to so they are phased in over time. As suggested in Chapter 4,
for many students with ASD it is ideal to begin employment and leisure
changes during the final years of high school. Then, after graduation,
once the individual has adjusted to employment and leisure activities
as the primary sources of daily activities, the family can consider making a change in living arrangements.

Adjusting to a Move Out of the Family Home

If your adult child with an ASD is moving into an assisted living
arrangement, the trained staff in those facilities can help you determine the appropriate pace for changing the home environment. For
example, they might recommend that your child begin by eating one
meal a day at the residence to get used to the other residents; or by
spending one weekend there to start and increasing time as your child
feels comfortable. How quickly you try to transition your adult child to
the new home may depend not only on her own ability to understand
what is happening, resistance to change, etc., but also on the other
residents' needs for gradual change.

Many of the visual supports discussed in Chapter 5, such as Social
Stories, can be useful in helping your child adjust to this change. For
example, she might benefit from a Social Story that clarifies that she
will still be allowed to visit you at home and how frequently she can
do so after she moves to her new residence.

Adjusting to College Life

If your adult child is moving into a college dorm or apartment, it will be important to structure the move so that she has control and feels safe. It may be important for your child to spend some extra time on campus before classes start getting used to the new living arrangement. If there is a Disability Services office, they may be able to help you coordinate this. Some college students with ASD might benefit from watching videos about the college and campus life there.

Your family and your college student with an ASD will need to determine parameters for contacting each other in order to promote independence for your child while still allowing her to feel safe. More frequent contact and visits may be appropriate in the beginning with goals for decreasing the contact over time. For example, you may determine that your child will call you once in the morning when she gets up and once in the evening each day. You can then decrease the amount of time for each call and then the frequency of the calls. Given that most college student text or email parents frequently from school, you may not want to limit this unless this type of contact is interfering with school work and social times.

Remaining in the Family Home after High School

If your adult child with ASD is remaining in the family home, you will need to decide how to continue to promote your child's independence. How will things at home be different now that your child has completed high school and is officially an adult? Issues to consider include:

- Do you need to establish new boundaries? For example, if your adult child is capable of going out on her own, does she need a curfew? Or, if she no longer needs to get up early for school, do you need to enforce a quiet time at night so others can sleep? See Chapter 5 for examples of visual supports that can help your child learn new household rules.
- Do you need to charge your adult child rent? Depending on what kind of government assistance she is receiving, you may need to charge her rent, board, or both. If you need to charge her rent, do you need to help her set money aside to pay it?

- Do you want to change the *chores* and other household responsibilities assigned to your child? In general, it is a good idea to gradually give your adult child increasing responsibilities, working systematically to teach her as many daily living tasks as possible and to reduce her reliance on family members.
- As more attention is being paid to opportunities for adults with ASD, assist your young adult in continuing to seek opportunities for leisure activities, social skills instruction, or behavior therapy.

Day-to-Day Activities: Structured Time

A seamless transition plan from school to adulthood leads directly from a structured school day to a structured school, work, or leisure setting following the completion of high school. Often, however, these plans do not translate to reality as intended. A stark reality for parents is that now they are the *case managers* for their adult children with autism. There are many considerations that need to be taken into account:

- transportation to and from work or the recreational activity,
- access to meals and snacks during the day (will your child pack her lunch? who will make it for her?),
- initial strategies to acclimate your child with autism to the setting prior to starting,
- orienting your child to the location and use of restrooms and break rooms, and
- familiarizing your child with the daily schedule itself.

Depending on the amount of support available to your adult child in the setting, many of these considerations must be resolved by you. For example, if your son or daughter will spend the day in an adult leisure center, you will need to ask what types of clothing and supplies need to be sent in. When your child was in school, school staff typically took care of such details and sent home lists of items for you to purchase and send to the school. If your adult child will be working in a supported employment setting, you may need to discuss a special diet or perhaps a toileting schedule. Adults with autism who are capable of competitive employment or postsecondary education will have acquired some independent problem-solving strategies. Yet, as stated earlier, they may still need support from other adults as they navigate the real world for the first time.

It is important to remember that neurotypical young adults often leave high school believing that they want to work in a specific field or study a certain topic. Then, they change their minds two or three times before they settle in on a focus area. The same may be true for the person with an ASD. Such unsettled times present a great deal of stress for all families. Stress is likely to be at a higher level, however, for families of young adults with autism who are undecided about their future.

If your adult child with autism is unsure about future plans, how you respond to her is critical. You will need to seek out supports in your community for help with changing your child's chosen path. For example, you may be able to get assistance from a "supports coordinator" at your local MH/MR or Developmental Disablities program. You should also seek support for yourself as discussed on page 94.

Day-to-Day Activities: Unstructured Time

Once students leave the structure of a school setting with built-in opportunities for leisure activities, it can be difficult to find good activities to help fill up unstructured time. As recommended in Chapter 4, you and the IEP team can work as partners to try out different types of leisure activities that your child can do both inside and outside of the home. In the final two years of school, your child can focus more on activities that are available in the community and less on those offered in school.

Balancing community involvement and leisure time activities with other schedules is a challenge for everyone whether they have a disability or not. For the person with autism, this challenge has some variables that may tip the balance one way or another. For young adults who are attending school or are employed but wish to participate in social activities with peers, it may be difficult to ensure that social activities do not interfere with school or work obligations.

One reason is that some people with ASDs have a skewed perception of expectations. They may believe that in order to maintain a relationship with people, they must participate in every activity the group does. Conversely, they may believe that work or school friends need to remain in those settings and that spending time with them in other settings is inappropriate. Your adult child with ASD may need you or another adult to help her understand such scenarios and may need to continue with social skills instructional strategies that were effective during the school years. Again, using visual supports such as Social Stories, Comic Strip Conversations, or video modeling, as discussed in Chapter 5, may help your adult child understand social expectations.

People with autism who require more support to participate in community and leisure activities may be dependent on others and their schedules for participation. It is important to seek out support from the community to allow young adults with ASD to spend time outside of their living quarters. For example, if your adult child is active in church activities, another church member might be willing to transport her. The same could be true for any type of organized event such as a bowling league, video club, or dancing group.

If your adult child needs adult help to participate in community activities, it will generally be your responsibility to find a volunteer to assist your child. (The exception is with activities such as Special Olympics or recreational activities run by your county or state that must provide assistance, as required by the Americans with Disabilities Act, to enable people with disabilities to participate.) Any volunteers you find to assist your adult child with autism will likely require training, which, again, you may need to provide.

Living Arrangements

Once your adult child with ASD has moved out of your home, you must ensure that your child or those who will be overseeing her welfare have all of the information needed to ensure her safety and well-being. After caring for your child for the first 18 to 21 years of her life, you will undoubtedly have many emotions stirring within when she leaves home, and you may have trouble focusing on her needs. Once again, having support through this transition is essential. You may be able to get support from former members of your child's IEP team, including agency personnel, financial planners, physicians, attorneys, and, if appropriate, college housing personnel. This is another time to connect with support groups for people with ASDs. There is no reason to make this journey alone. If you can find out how another family with similar experiences has coped, it may help you cope with your own child's transition.

As stated earlier in the book, living arrangements outside the home are, unfortunately, limited. Just because there may be few living options for people with ASD in your community, however, does not mean that your adult child's safety and well-being should be sacrificed. Once she has moved into a new living arrangement, you must vigilantly monitor the situation to make sure her living area is clean and that there are no concerns about environmental, physical, and emotional safety. If you have any concerns about these areas, you will need to be prepared to immediately remove your adult child from the home environment and make a report to the appropriate authorities.

Troubleshooting

No matter how well you plan for your child's transition during the school years, unforeseen problems are likely to crop up once she is out in the real world. The best place to look for support in solving these problems is generally at an agency designed for people with intellectual disabilities or developmental disabilities. Agencies specifically for adults with autism spectrum disorders are in their early stages and may or may not be available in your geographic area.

The chart that follows lists some common scenarios that may arise and suggestions for starting points to begin dealing with the circumstances. Please remember that information in this section may not be relevant to every scenario. Rather, it is meant to **guide** the parents of adults with ASDs.

Concluding Thoughts

We have spent some time in this chapter discussing how to plan for unforeseen circumstances. Although it is good to be prepared for problems, if they do arise, you also need to consider that the transition plan that you developed in high school may be right on target and may require only minimal adjustments for bumps in the road.

Remember to celebrate successes. Share the success stories with members of your child's team, with agency personnel, and with other families who have young adults with autism spectrum disorders—or better yet, with those who still have students in middle school or high school. Let others learn and take heart from hearing about strategies that worked for you and your son or daughter.

Troubleshooting Post-High School Situations for Young Adults with Autism		
	Situation	**Underlying Need or Cause**	**Starting Point**
Job or Postsecondary Education Program	■ Adult with ASD is struggling with expectations in setting	■ Lacks prerequisite skills ■ Not enough supports	■ Explore opportunities for training or tutoring, including the addition of a job coach ■ Make sure needed accommodations are in place
	■ Refusing to complete tasks	■ Lacks prerequisite skills ■ Demands are too intense or the adult doesn't understand tasks ■ Doesn't understand what to do ■ Lacks motivation and/or is bored	■ Explore opportunities for training or tutoring ■ Explore tasks and request task analysis to further break down skills ■ Incorporate reinforcement using passions or strengths
	■ Refusing to attend school or go to work	■ Problem with transportation ■ Schedule is too demanding ■ Dislikes the job or educational program ■ Is being bullied or abused or feels anxious for unknown reason ■ Finds the situation confusing or overwhelming	■ Explore transportation supports or alternatives ■ Inquire about more frequent breaks, mixing tasks, or decreasing time at setting ■ Try to find out from the person what is wrong ■ Try to determine who is involved or the source of anxiety ■ Help determine additional supports that may assist the person with ASD

(continued on next page)

(continued from previous page)

Situation	Underlying Need or Cause	Starting Point
■ Wants to change schools or employment	■ Could be any of the above ■ The job or school is not what the person thought it would be	■ Use social skills strategies to discover and then to process reason for desiring a change ■ Conduct observations; speak to coworkers or teachers (with the adult's permission) ■ Seek assistance from agency or school personnel ■ Explore alternative options
Leisure Time ■ Too much down time	■ Lacks community or leisure involvement ■ Structured activities are not available locally	■ Explore community opportunities to match activities with interests and passions ■ Create opportunities through support group connections ■ Look for opportunities in nearby town
■ Young adult with autism asked to leave organized group	■ Inappropriate behaviors and/or interactions ■ Organization members do not understand ASD or how to provide accommodations	■ Seek assistance from an agency such as MH/MR to continue educating student in these areas ■ Work to help them become educated about ASD and possible accommodations
■ Difficulty traveling to and from activities	■ Lacks independent safety and navigation skills ■ Does not have enough money for bus fare, etc.	■ Seek assistance from an agency such as MH/MR with teaching safety and navigation skills

		Feels anxious about transportation method, contact with passengers, etc.	■ Look for adult volunteer or caregiver to assist with transportation ■ Explore discounts for transportation or special transportation from bus or taxi companies ■ Explore special community transportation from bus or taxi companies
	■ Fixates on one activity or refuses to try alternate activities	■ Feels safe with preferred activities	■ Reinforce time spent on alternate activities or pair a new activity with a preferred activity or person
	■ Funding needed for support falls through	■ In control of government	■ Follow grievance procedure if one exists ■ Seek assistance from agencies and financial planner ■ Brainstorm with other families who are in same situation
Living Arrangements	■ Lengthy waiting list for supported living	■ Not enough settings to support growing need for services	■ Develop plan to help person maintain or improve independent living skills until opening arises ■ Seek other options that may be a little further away from home ■ Work with support group and agencies to explore opening new homes ■ Consider moving to another area

(continued on next page)

(continued from previous page)

Situation	Underlying Need or Cause	Starting Point
■ Not enough supports and accommodations provided for campus housing	■ Supports and accommodations required exceed those available from resident counselors ■ Student needs more support than expected ■ College promised more support than it is able to provide	■ Seek a local adult who is willing to mentor the young adult with autism ■ Look for an alternate school that can provide accommodations ■ Have student temporarily commute from home
■ Disagreements between parents and service providers about what is best for the young adult	■ Philosophies and goals are different	■ Maintain open dialogue and seek compromise ■ Seek an impartial and objective mediator to assist, perhaps a legal advisor or clergy person
■ Can't get along with housemate or support staff ■ Cannot or will not perform necessary housekeeping or cooking tasks	■ Lacks social skills ■ Lacks necessary skills or motivation ■ Does not comprehend consequences ■ Needs are not being met; trying to communicate something; or wants to escape tasks	■ Provide social skills instruction through role playing; use visual supports such as Social Stories (Chapter 4) ■ Break down skills into component parts and reinforce completion ■ Provide safety training and strategies for mapping out consequences of different choices

■ Individual is making unwise choices related to safety, food, or activities ■ Behavior or skills are regressing ■ Person seems anxious or depressed	■ May be overwhelmed with day-to-day tasks, living arrangements, or relationships, or may have underlying medical problem	■ Work with agency mental health personnel such as a psychologist to determine the function of the behavior ■ Work with agency mental health personnel such as a psychologist to determine the function of the behavior; consult physician; consider counseling or medication

7 | Putting It All Together

Over the past six chapters, we have reviewed a wide array of guidelines and resources that can be incorporated into the transition process for your student with an autism spectrum disorder. We realize that at times the compilation and practical application of so much information can be overwhelming. To make it easier for you to put all of these ideas into practice, we have developed a schematic tool to help you apply the ideas to your specific student. Afterwards, we describe four very different students with autism spectrum disorders and their experiences as they transitioned from school to adult life. Reading about their experiences will hopefully give you a better understanding of how you can "put it all together."

Transition Portfolio Planning Tool

In Chapter 4, we suggested that families take ownership of a transition portfolio for their child. Given the number of areas for which information must be kept, we thought it would be helpful to have a tool that provides an overview or summary of transition planning. Each section of the chart provides an area for recording the goal for each transition area, what must be done, and notes for future reference.

Using the questions from each phase of transition described in Chapter 4, and the year for each annual IEP, each student and/or his parents or guardians should complete and subsequently update the summary for that year. It will be helpful to do this around the same time each year. An example showing how one year of each phase might be filled out for a student with ASD follows at the end of this chapter. You can find a blank transition planning tool in the Appendix.

Transition Experiences of Students with ASD

William

William is a young man with moderate autism who received special education services throughout his educational career. Although he started out in self-contained classes for students with autism, by middle school he was assigned to a "learning support" classroom which included students with varying developmental disabilities who had mild to moderate learning delays.

As William entered ninth grade, his parents and the educational staff began to seriously discuss transition issues. One of the major goals initially was to revisit William's IEP goals and weed out the goals that no longer made sense. For example, William had been struggling in math for years. In fact, he often behaved inappropriately during math instruction (e.g., yelling and running out of the classroom). As a consequence, the transition team started to question the validity of teaching him how to perform higher level math tasks such as two- or three-digit addition and subtraction problems. At one point, William's teacher noted that she personally relied exclusively on a calculator for real-life activities that required math (e.g., balancing her checkbook, adding up the total of purchases at the grocery store). One by one, each transition team member acknowledged that they also used a calculator for these types of tasks. It quickly became apparent that this should be William's goal as well.

Other IEP goals that focused on higher-level academic skills but would have little functional use in William's day-to-day routine as an adult were also taken out of the IEP. Eventually, the document included only attainable, functional skills. Wiliam blossomed as he progressed on these goals, and he was very successful in his freshman and sophomore years of high school.

When William was in tenth grade, the school's job trainer began to assess his skills, needs, and interests. After observing William many times and interviewing him and people who knew him well, the job trainer gained a better understanding of work settings that might make sense. Throughout tenth and eleventh grade, William participated in work crews that went into the community one day per week to complete a variety of activities such as boxing pizzas at a local pizzeria, sorting clothes at a local mission, and cleaning dishes at a restaurant.

William consistently enjoyed the work at the restaurant, and his job was even expanded to include some simple food preparation tasks. Fortunately, the owner of the restaurant had a nephew with autism, so he was especially open to the idea of hiring an employee with autism. William's teacher, Mrs. Ryan, visited the restaurant at the beginning of his senior year. She and the job trainer worked together to develop specific instructional strategies that would help William be successful working in a restaurant. William's speech therapist also got involved and generated specific speech goals based upon the communication skills William would need within the restaurant setting. These strategies were then implemented across both school and work settings in order to help William generalize his new skills effectively.

During his senior year, William began attending school three days a week and worked at the restaurant the other two days with the assistance of a job coach. Over time, William worked an increasing number of days at the restaurant as his schedule at school was faded. By the end of his senior year, William was working four days a week at the restaurant, and he became a full-time employee the week following his high school graduation.

The transition team realized that William would probably continue to need a job coach at the restaurant. However, once he was no longer a student, the funding for his school-based job coach would be discontinued. William's parents had anticipated this problem prior to his graduation, and had therefore explored new funding sources. Fortunately, they found a community agency that provided ongoing job support for adults with developmental disabilities. Although the switch from his school-based job coach to his new one was a bit difficult for William at first, the consistent use of familiar, specially designed instructional tools that had been shared across agencies helped him tolerate the change. William and the transition team were overall quite pleased with his "launching" into a career.

In considering living arrangements for William, his parents recognized that he would need ongoing supervision for the rest of his life. They were uncomfortable, however, with the idea of him living in a setting run by "strangers." Therefore, they had had numerous discussions over the years with their older daughter, Mary, about the possibility of William living with her once they could no longer care for him. Mary was very receptive to the idea and William was clearly attached to Mary. By the time William graduated from high school, Mary was in her mid-twenties and married. Her husband was well acquainted with William and was comfortable with the thought of William eventually moving into their home; in fact, he had helped to refurbish an extra room in the house to create a bedroom just for William.

For the time being, William's parents want him to continue living with them. However, since they know that change is difficult for William, they have arranged his schedule so that he spends every Wednesday and every other weekend at his sister's home. This gives William's parents some free time to explore their own interests, while providing an opportunity for William to get used to day-to-day life at his sister's home. All in all, William and his family have been satisfied with the way William's transition into adulthood has gone.

Frannie

Frannie is a twenty-three-year-old woman with "high functioning" autism. During elementary and middle school, she attended special education classes, but spent increasing time in inclusion. As she finished middle school, her IEP team began to focus specifically on developing a transition plan for Frannie once she graduated from high school. Due to her strong intellectual skills and interest in attending college, all agreed that this should be the overall goal.

The transition team felt that Frannie was ready to attend general education classes full time once she reached high school. To help assure her success, the team decided to provide her with the support of weekly consultations with an itinerant teacher specializing in students with autism. The itinerant consultant held individual meetings with Frannie to teach her about organizational and social-emotional regulation techniques, and also provided suggestions to her regular education teachers to assure that they were consistently using specialized instructional approaches. (For example, she recommended they use visual supports such as a written daily schedule and reminders and let Frannie take tests in a separate room.) Frannie was also allowed to complete school projects on her own at times when her peers were doing group projects, since working on group projects notably increased her anxiety level. Although she continued to be a loner while at school, Frannie was generally content and graduated from high school with a 3.4 grade point average.

Frannie's parents were proud and optimistic, especially when she was accepted at a local, moderately competitive college which allowed her to continue living at home. Unfortunately, the summer before her freshman year at college, she read a newspaper article about a bomb that had exploded at a college in another state. As is true for most individuals with autism, Frannie had a tendency to perseverate on certain topics, and she became preoccupied with this association between colleges and bombs. She became highly concerned that colleges were dangerous places and often talked about these fears. Although she began attending the local university in the fall, she was soon having panic attacks in class and her grades were suffering.

Frannie's parents and priest attempted to reason with her to decrease her anxiety. However, it became clear that she needed professional help. Fortunately, the college's guidance staff included a young woman who was well-trained in the use of cognitive behavior therapy for anxiety disorders. More importantly, she had experience working with students on the autism spectrum. Although Frannie continued to experience periodic bouts of anxiety and various "quirky" behaviors related to having autism, she was eventually able to return to her classes full time, thanks to weekly therapy sessions and anti-anxiety medication. She graduated in five years with exemplary grades with a degree in meteorology (weather having been one of her passions since she was a small girl).

Although Frannie had hoped to become a television meteorologist when she was younger, guidance from both her family and counselor had helped her realize that this goal was unrealistic due to her continued difficulties during social situations. Instead, she explored other types of employment related to her studies. Fortunately, a family friend had worked at a local airport for many years and was able to recommend Frannie for a position involving weather analysis and reporting to assist with scheduling flights. This position involved recording incoming weather information and conveying the data in writing to other airline staff, and so did not tax Frannie's social skills. The family friend served as Frannie's mentor, giving her valuable advice about getting along with colleagues and adapting to work conventions at the airport workplace. All agreed that Frannie had been successfully "launched" into a career!

Once Frannie's employment situation was going so well, everyone agreed that it was time to consider finding her own living arrangement.

Frannie expressed a strong desire to live on her own without any room-mates, so a single apartment seemed to be her best option. With some assistance from her parents, she wrote a list of preferred criteria for a potential apartment: 1) it had to be within walking distance of the airport, since she did not want to learn to drive a car and did not want to be dependent upon someone else for a ride to or from work; 2) it could not be on the first floor because she was worried about the possibility of intruders breaking into a first floor apartment; and 3) the rental fee, including utilities, had to be a third of her monthly salary or less.

Frannie used this checklist when reviewing the classified ads in the local paper in search of a single-bedroom apartment. Within a month, she was able to find an apartment that matched her criteria. Although she was a bit anxious initially, with the support of her parents and mentor she was soon able to function quite independently with only periodic assistance.

Paul

Paul, twenty-two, has Asperger's disorder. Although his intelligence had been tested in the superior range, Paul had a chronic history of social and emotional concerns that had severely limited his ability to perform well in school. As is typical for individuals with Asperger's disorder, Paul's perception of the world was very rule-bound according to his own set of do's and don'ts. For example, he felt it was "illogical" to take a test if he had already been tested on the material in the past. As a result, he received 0 points on various tests of previously assessed skills. He was also especially sensitive to being perceived as different compared to his peers, so he would actively avoid any resource or auxiliary support that was deemed "special education." By the time Paul finished ninth grade, he was often found aimlessly walking the school hallways and he had a 2.0 grade average.

The transition team met at the beginning of Paul's tenth grade year to revisit his transition plan. Because of Paul's obvious intellectual abilities, his parents had always assumed that he would attend college once he graduated from high school. However, it had become clear that this was most likely an unrealistic goal after all, due to Paul's severe rigidity of thought. As the team discussed options, they noted that the only topic that maintained Paul's interest was computers. Indeed, one of his favorite pastimes was buying old computers and revamping them. In fact, everyone agreed that Paul was actually quite talented in this area. The team decided to take advantage of this passion and suggest that Paul attend a local vocational program where he could earn a certificate in computer technology.

When this option was presented to him, Paul was highly enthusiastic. During tenth and eleventh grade, Paul attended the vocational program for half the day and regular education classes at the public high school for the other half. Supportive services were provided in a discreet manner so that Paul did not feel "different"; for example, his social skills instruction was conducted in the gym during a study hall period so that his peers no longer saw him entering the guidance office. Also, the special education staff who visited with Paul at school began taking off their ID badges when they worked with him in order to decrease the possibility that peers would perceive him as a special education student.

By the end of Paul's eleventh grade year, it was increasingly evident that Paul was finding his regular education classes "meaningless" due to his disinterest in the topics discussed. No amount of reasoning by his parents or support staff could change his mind and he continued to just barely pass these subjects. The transition team finally agreed to honor Paul's preference to stop taking general education classes at the high school. That summer, his job trainer found a part-time internship for computer programmers at a local electronics business. During his senior year of high school, Paul attended vocational school in the mornings and worked at the electronics business in the afternoons. He finished his high school career with a certificate in computer programming, and his work at the electronics business was increased to full-time status.

Since Paul was earning a relatively decent wage as a computer programmer, he voiced the wish to move out of the family home. His parents realized that Paul was not quite ready to live on his own, but respected his desire for increased independence. They contacted the local county agency serving adults with developmental disabilities and set up an appointment. When Paul and his parents met with the county case manager, they learned that there was funding available to support adults with autism spectrum disorders within a supervised apartment setting. They visited the apartment complex and were impressed with the staff. Paul met his potential roommate and was glad to hear that he was also a computer game enthusiast. Over the next few months, Paul visited the apartment more and more often, then finally moved in. He was clearly excited about being on his own.

Paul's parents were initially anxious about his new-found independence, but they continued to monitor the situation to assure that he was receiving sufficient support and was making ongoing progress. In addition, the supervised apartment staff checked in on the roommates on a daily basis to assist with financial, emotional, or other areas of daily living. Over time, everyone breathed a sigh of relief over Paul's successful "launching."

Mike

Mr. and Mrs. Martinelli had always been involved in every step of their son's education. Mike had been diagnosed with both mental retardation and autism at a young age and had required ongoing special education and intensive instruction from the day he entered early intervention services. Because of Mike's very limited communication skills, the Martinellis were especially aware of their need to advocate for their son's needs.

Over the years, Mike had shown slow but steady progress on many IEP goals. He had learned to perform most daily living skills independently and was able to use a few signs to communicate his basic wishes. When Mike reached adolescence, the Martinellis and the school staff began to focus on transition in order to assure that he would be as ready as possible once he graduated from high school. Due to his significant delays, the Martinellis already knew that they would be choosing to have Mike remain in school until age 21. Nonetheless, considering his slow pace of learning, they also realized that transition plans needed to be made as soon as possible.

When Mike entered middle school, the Martinellis participated in a series of PATH meetings (see Chapter 3). During these meetings, a group of people who knew Mike well—including school, community, and family members—discussed his preferences, dislikes, skills, and needs. Many questions were generated regarding Mike's future, and the team chose certain high priority goals to be accomplished within a designated time-frame. For example, the team decided that Mike needed to learn a wider variety of independent leisure activities (he tended to spend his free time engaged in self-stimulatory behaviors). As is true for many people with autism spectrum disorders, Mike often found crowds and commotion to be overwhelming, so the team determined that he also needed to learn to tolerate being in the community. The team worked together to develop creative ways to improve Mike's skills in these areas.

The needs and strengths outlined by the PATH process were incorporated into Mike's IEP goals as well as the interventions used in the home by his parents and a community-funded caretaker who worked in the home three evenings per week. The team met every three months to assure that the goals outlined during the PATH were maintained as a focus and modified as needed. Most importantly, these meetings allowed the entire transition team to share ideas and insights with each other regarding Mike's future.

Everyone on the transition team agreed that Mike would find even the most basic work setting to be too difficult. Instead, the team decided that Mike's future would involve a recreation-based day program. As a consequence, Mike began receiving community-based instruction in which he would visit various sites in the neighborhood in order to learn how to respond in these settings. By graduation day, Mike could participate in a wide variety of recreational activities such as bowling, going to baseball games, and taking walks in the park. The team was especially gratified that he had learned to tolerate crowds due to their intensive efforts and specially designed instruction.

During his high school years, Mike's parents began to network with other parents of young adults with developmental disabilities. They explored the funding options available after high school and were disheartened to find that there were long waiting lists for basic resources such as group homes or day programs.

The Martinellis met two other couples who were equally frustrated with the limited services available for their children with autism, and the three couples started thinking creatively about the situation. They decided that they would pool their own money and buy a group home designed especially for their three sons. Soon after the sons graduated from high school at age 21, the parents bought a small house in their hometown. They then joined forces with a local service agency that had sufficient backing and funds to pay staff, but insufficient monies to buy a home. The parents and agency oversaw the creation of a highly personalized living arrangement for all three young men. Since all three men required 24-hour supervision and assistance, the project was time-consuming. However, with all three couples and the already-established agency working together, the work was manageable.

Between his new home and his daily recreational activities with a local social service agency, Mike seemed to thoroughly enjoy his launching into adulthood.

Transition Portfolio Planning Tool for Students with Autism Spectrum Disorders

Demographics

Name: Chris Martin

Date of Birth: 2/14/93

Street Address: 1000 Main St.

Telephone: 555-0000

City/State/Zip: Yourtown, YS 00000

Email: cml23@yahool.com

Support Network

Family Contacts/Roles: Parents/Guardians: Frank and Michelle Martin

Sister: Bridgett (h) 555-0000; (w) 555-1234

Agency/Medical/Financial/Legal: Office of Developmental Disabilities Mr. D.: 555-2222

Dr. T. Giraldi (medical): 222-0101

Dr. J. Allan (psychiatrist): 222-0011

Attorney P. Jackson (finances and legal): 211-5000

	Strengths	Accommodations
Communication	Shares needs/wants	Assistive device—Dynavox
Social Interaction	Participates when prompted	Uses Dynavox with adult support
Rigid Interests/ Passions	Movies; planes	Watches sections of a movie about planes as a reinforcer for complying with academic tasks
Activities of Daily Living	Independent toileting Minimal assistance at meals	Needs food cut and drinks with straw Uses micro-schedule—visual support with BoardMaker symbols for each step of the toileting and grooming process

EARLY PHASE: Independence

Focus Area: Expressive Communication	Focus Area: Receptive Communication	Focus Area: Social Interaction
Year One	**Year One**	**Year One**
Goal: Communicate without prompting	**Goal:** Respond to directions	**Goal:** Play card game during free time using device to communicate
Must Do: Program Dynavox—parent/ teacher/speech therapist	**Must Do:** Work on same directions at home and school	**Must Do:** Communicate with school about games played at home
Notes: Chris is communicating requests for food, movies without prompt!	**Notes:**	**Notes:** Inconsistent—interacts with adults at school and parents and cousin at home, but not peers at school

Focus Area: Rigid Interests/Passions	Focus Area: Activities of Daily Living
Year One	**Year One**
Goal: Watch movies during free time rather than watching them as a reinforcer contingent on work completion	**Goal:** Independently get lunch in school cafeteria
Must Do: Be consistent—home and school	**Must Do:** Use similar procedure in fast food settings outside of school
Notes: This strategy works best when C. has airplane or movie magazines to look at for reinforcement	**Notes:**

MIDDLE PHASE: Match Abilities/Interests to Outcomes

Focus Area: Postsecondary Education	Focus Area: Employment	Focus Area: Living Arrangements
Year One	**Year One**	**Year One**
Goal: Advocate for self **Must Do:** Provide instruction on using Dynavox to advocate for needs **Notes:** Stating when ill, hungry, tired	**Goal:** Follow two-step directions with visual prompt **Must Do:** Create visual prompts for home **Notes:** Visual supports working for grooming and toileting—slow progress with independent tasks to build skills such as "put in" and categorizing	**Goal:** Perform basic activities of daily living including choosing items off a grocery shelf using visual supports and cleaning up after eating **Must Do:** Provide list of common items purchased at store; Get on group home list just in case **Notes:** Needs support focusing on item on shelf

Focus Area: Community Involvement/Leisure & Recreational Activities	Focus Area: Interagency Involvement	
Year One	**Year One**	
Goal: Watch a movie at a movie theater **Must Do:** Take advantage of times when movies of interest are at theater **Notes:** Prefers animation to real life	**Goal:** Match goals in IEP to Behavior Support goals used by the in-home agency personnel **Must Do:** Include behavior support staff and Transition Support Services in all school meetings and vice versa Focus on Office of Developmental Disabilities for supports (starting in January) **Notes:** TSS services discontinued in January	

LATER PHASE: Life Outcomes

Focus Area: Postsecondary Education	Focus Area: Employment	Focus Area: Living Arrangements
Year One	**Year One**	**Year One**
Goal: Not applicable	**Goal:** Use a picture schedule showing each step of a task to complete work tasks	**Goal:** Increase independence in all activities of daily living by decreasing each prompt level at least one level.
Must Do:	**Must Do:** Create work boxes and visual schedules for each task (school)	**Must Do:** Ask group home provider to come to house and do assessment
Notes:	**Notes:** Connect with Yourtown Rehab Services for task suggestions and assessment	**Notes:** Talked with financial advisor about trust for C.

Focus Area: Community Involvement/Leisure & Recreational Activities	Focus Area: Interagency Involvement
Year One	**Year One**
Goal: Choose a movie to attend by watching trailers on the Internet	**Goal:** Work with Office of Developmental Disabilities to link with support agencies for after school—especially Office of Vocational Rehabilitation
Must Do:	**Must Do:**
Notes:	**Notes:** Explore supported employment opportunities

8 | Final Advice for the Journey

As the television commercial notes, "Life comes at you fast." If you are not diligent and proactive, your student with an autism spectrum disorder will be nearing graduation before you know it and you will be scrambling to develop a transition plan. Hopefully, this book has convinced you of the need to address transition issues early and often, and has provided some clear guidelines that you can follow throughout the journey. Given a strong support system, dedicated transition team members, and a willingness to "think outside the box," we predict that your journey will be a successful one.

In closing, here are just a few more themes that we would like you to keep in mind.

"Change Is Okay"

As we all know, changes in routine or in the environment are highly stressful for many individuals with autism spectrum disorders. One student with an autism spectrum disorder may have a meltdown because an assembly has preempted math class, while another may become overly distraught if the living room couch is replaced. We have spent hours upon hours teaching students with ASDs that "change is okay" via strategies such as Social Stories™, videomodeling, and cognitive restructuring techniques.

Although students with autism spectrum disorders sometimes seem to have extreme reactions to change, most people (typically developing or not) find change to be disconcerting. Just as we teach our students to accept changes in their lives, we must us all recognize that life is dynamic and ever-changing. We have all gone through times when we have had to adapt to new living situations, job changes, or even familial changes such as a divorce. Although the initial phase of adapting can be somewhat anxiety-provoking, in the end we all learn to adjust and sometimes the changes actually lead to notable improvements in our lives.

Similarly, everyone involved with the transition plan has to recognize that time is passing, whether we want it to or not, and therefore our student with an ASD is growing into a young adult. Accepting this fact can be especially difficult for parents of individuals with autism spectrum disorders because they perceive their children as especially vulnerable and in need of protection. However, given appropriate supports and ongoing strategies, adults with ASDs can become productive, relatively independent members of society.

Rather than perceiving the changes inherent to transition as frightening, try to "let go." Instead, recognize how very exciting such a time can be for your young adult with an ASD. If you are finding it particularly difficult to let go, it is often helpful to talk to other parents who have already gone through the process, attend a local support group, or seek individual counseling from a therapist who fully understands the myriad of emotions you may be feeling.

Dealing with the Emotional Roller Coaster of Transition

As with most of life's experiences, the transition process involves both highs and lows. There will be times when an idea seems brilliant and the transition team becomes exhilarated, and other times when the inevitable obstacles that occur during any transition process seem insurmountable. Parents and professionals alike can find this emotional roller coaster discouraging and exhausting.

The most effective strategy to combat these reactions is to *keep your eye on the goal.* If one route is not working, find another. Add new team members if necessary to provide the necessary knowledge or support service. Create a mid-step to jumpstart the process when you reach a plateau. For example, you might need to arrange for a new mentor to provide guidance for your child or break down the current step into more manageable tasks. Contact parents whose children with autism spectrum disorders have successfully transitioned from high school and ask for their insights. If you do not know anyone who has been through this before, join a local parent support group to see if any of the members can assist you. If you are feeling especially overwhelmed, anxious, or depressed, it might make sense to seek counseling to help you over the emotional hump. Most importantly, recognize that these ups and downs are just part of the process and allow yourself to relax.

Do Not Become Complacent

It is all too common for parents and professionals to become complacent either during the transition process or once the student with an ASD has graduated and entered adulthood. However, remember that these young people, like the rest of us, are a "work in progress." Continue to develop techniques to expand the young adult's communication and social skills. For example, if your adult child can speak in abbreviated sentences, prompt her to use full ones. If she has developed a friendship with one person, see if you can help her develop another with a new acquaintance.

Sometimes the overall slope of learning may be somewhat dampened once the individual with an ASD reaches adulthood. Still, there are always new and exciting skills to be considered which could result in still farther expansion of her day-to-day experience. "Education" does not end when a person with an ASD graduates from high school.

Continue to Focus on Increasing Independence

Most adults with autism spectrum disorders need some level of support throughout their lives. However, they have the right to be as autonomous as possible, whether in the workplace or in their home. Increasing their ability to be independent boosts their feelings of self-confidence, decreases the need for anyone to intrude on their privacy, and can open up new opportunities for living, working, or recreation. Therefore, continue to explore ways in which your young adult child with an ASD can become more independent, even in the most minor of ways. Make sure that everyone involved in supporting your child also values and promotes independence (e.g., group home staff, employers). Periodic team meetings to discuss progress in this area will assure that your child's skills do not plateau.

If your grown child is able to live successfully on her own, this can pose some unique problems if you feel there are still areas that need attention. For example, if you think that your grown child should have a more active social life, you can subtly encourage ways in which this can happen. However, as with all parents whose grown children are now off on their own, you need to honor your child's preferences. Perhaps an active social life is more important to *you* than to your grown child, and therefore you need to refrain from putting pressure on your son or daughter

Future Transitions

Most parents and support staff breathe a huge sigh of relief once their son or daughter with an ASD is settled in the adult world. However, the job of being a parent is never truly finished, especially when your offspring has a developmental disability. This is not to imply that parents should feel forever tethered to their adult child's treatment program. But it is inevitable that future transitions will occur due to unforeseen circumstances. These changes could involve issues *external* to your child with an ASD, such as reallocations of state/federal funding, staff turnover, roommate switches, etc. They could also be due to *internal* changes within her, such as new passions or skills, new friendships or romances, or health problems.

Regardless of the impetus for any future transitions, the strategies that have been discussed in this book should be useful in helping your adult child adapt to change. For example, you can use the techniques outlined in Chapter 5 to involve your child in the transition, and you can use the strategies discussed in Chapter 3 to help develop a new transition team to support your family and your child through the next phase in his or her life. Life is a dynamic process and we need an effective set of tools to respond to it successfully. Hopefully, the ideas provided in this book will make it easier for you and your child to navigate through the challenges and opportunities that arise both during and after his or her "launching" into adulthood.

Appendix

**Transition Portfolio Planning Tool
for Students with
Autism Spectrum Disorders**

Transition Portfolio Planning Tool for Students with Autism Spectrum Disorders

Demographics

Name: _____   Date of Birth: _____

Street Address: _____   Telephone: _____

City/State/Zip: _____   Email: _____

Support Network

Family Contacts/Roles: _____

_____

_____

_____

Agency/Medical/Financial/Legal: _____

_____

_____

_____

	Strengths	Accommodations
Communication		
Social Interaction		
Rigid Interests/ Passions		
Activities of Daily Living		

EARLY PHASE

Focus Area: Expressive Communication

Goal—Independence

Year One	Year Two	Year Three	Year Four
Goal:	Goal:	Goal:	Goal:
Must Do:	Must Do:	Must Do:	Must Do:
Notes:	Notes:	Notes:	Notes:
Goal:	Goal:	Goal:	Goal:
Must Do:	Must Do:	Must Do:	Must Do:
Notes:	Notes:	Notes:	Notes:

Focus Area: Receptive Communication

Year One	Year Two	Year Three	Year Four
Goal:	Goal:	Goal:	Goal:
Must Do:	Must Do:	Must Do:	Must Do:
Notes:	Notes:	Notes:	Notes:
Goal:	Goal:	Goal:	Goal:
Must Do:	Must Do:	Must Do:	Must Do:
Notes:	Notes:	Notes:	Notes:

Focus Area: Social Interaction			
Year One	**Year Two**	**Year Three**	**Year Four**
Goal:	Goal:	Goal:	Goal:
Must Do:	Must Do:	Must Do:	Must Do:
Notes:	Notes:	Notes:	Notes:
Goal:	Goal:	Goal:	Goal:
Must Do:	Must Do:	Must Do:	Must Do:
Notes:	Notes:	Notes:	Notes:

Focus Area: Rigid Interests/Passions

Year One	Year Two	Year Three	Year Four
Goal:	Goal:	Goal:	Goal:
Must Do:	Must Do:	Must Do:	Must Do:
Notes:	Notes:	Notes:	Notes:
Goal:	Goal:	Goal:	Goal:
Must Do:	Must Do:	Must Do:	Must Do:
Notes:	Notes:	Notes:	Notes:

Focus Area: Activities of Daily Living			
Year One	**Year Two**	**Year Three**	**Year Four**
Goal:	Goal:	Goal:	Goal:
Must Do:	Must Do:	Must Do:	Must Do:
Notes:	Notes:	Notes:	Notes:
Goal:	Goal:	Goal:	Goal:
Must Do:	Must Do:	Must Do:	Must Do:
Notes:	Notes:	Notes:	Notes:

MIDDLE PHASE Goals—Matching Abilities & Interests to Life Outcomes

Focus Area: Postsecondary Education

Year One	Year Two	Year Three
Goal:	Goal:	Goal:
Must Do:	Must Do:	Must Do:
Notes:	Notes:	Notes:
Goal:	Goal:	Goal:
Must Do:	Must Do:	Must Do:
Notes:	Notes:	Notes:

Focus Area: Employment			
Year One	**Year Two**	**Year Three**	
Goal:	Goal:	Goal:	
Must Do:	Must Do:	Must Do:	
Notes:	Notes:	Notes:	
Goal:	Goal:	Goal:	
Must Do:	Must Do:	Must Do:	
Notes:	Notes:	Notes:	

Focus Area: Living Arrangements		
Year One	**Year Two**	**Year Three**
Goal:	Goal:	Goal:
Must Do:	Must Do:	Must Do:
Notes:	Notes:	Notes:
Goal:	Goal:	Goal:
Must Do:	Must Do:	Must Do:
Notes:	Notes:	Notes:

Focus Area: Community Involvement/Leisure & Recreational Activities

Year One	Year Two	Year Three
Goal:	Goal:	Goal:
Must Do:	Must Do:	Must Do:
Notes:	Notes:	Notes:
Goal:	Goal:	Goal:
Must Do:	Must Do:	Must Do:
Notes:	Notes:	Notes:

Focus Area: Interagency Involvement		
Year One	**Year Two**	**Year Three**
Goal:	Goal:	Goal:
Must Do:	Must Do:	Must Do:
Notes:	Notes:	Notes:
Goal:	Goal:	Goal:
Must Do:	Must Do:	Must Do:
Notes:	Notes:	Notes:

LATER PHASE

Goals—Life Outcomes

Focus Area: Postsecondary Education

Year One	Year Two	Year Three
Goal:	Goal:	Goal:
Must Do:	Must Do:	Must Do:
Notes:	Notes:	Notes:
Goal:	Goal:	Goal:
Must Do:	Must Do:	Must Do:
Notes:	Notes:	Notes:

Focus Area: Employment		
Year One	**Year Two**	**Year Three**
Goal:	Goal:	Goal:
Must Do:	Must Do:	Must Do:
Notes:	Notes:	Notes:
Goal:	Goal:	Goal:
Must Do:	Must Do:	Must Do:
Notes:	Notes:	Notes:

Focus Area: Living Arrangements			
	Year One	Year Two	Year Three
	Goal:	Goal:	Goal:
	Must Do:	Must Do:	Must Do:
	Notes:	Notes:	Notes:
	Goal:	Goal:	Goal:
	Must Do:	Must Do:	Must Do:
	Notes:	Notes:	Notes:

Focus Area: Community Involvement/Leisure & Recreational Activities

Year One	Year Two	Year Three
Goal:	Goal:	Goal:
Must Do:	Must Do:	Must Do:
Notes:	Notes:	Notes:
Goal:	Goal:	Goal:
Must Do:	Must Do:	Must Do:
Notes:	Notes:	Notes:

Focus Area: Interagency Involvement		
Year One	**Year Two**	**Year Three**
Goal:	Goal:	Goal:
Must Do:	Must Do:	Must Do:
Notes:	Notes:	Notes:
Goal:	Goal:	Goal:
Must Do:	Must Do:	Must Do:
Notes:	Notes:	Notes:

Resource Guide

Transition Issues in General

Autism Source
www.autismsource.org
(Online referral database of the Autism Society of America lists local services, providers, and support.)

Institute for Community Inclusion
UMass Boston
100 Morrissey Blvd.
Boston, MA 02125
617-287-4300; 617-287-4352 (fax)
www.communityinclusion.org

Life Skills for Vocational Success
www.workshopsinc.com/manual

National Center on Secondary Education and Transition (NCSET)
Institute on Community Integration
University of Minnesota
6 Pattee Hall
Minneapolis, MN 55455
612-624-2097; 612-624-9344 (fax)
www.ncset.org

National Dissemination Center for Children with Disabilities (NICHY)
P.O. Box 1492
Washington, DC 20013
800-695-0285; 202-884-8441 (fax)
www.nichy.org
　　(Clicking on "Educate Children 3-22" and then "Transition to Adulthood" takes you to a myriad of parent-friendly, online publications on transition issues.)

Pacer Center
8161 Normandale Blvd.
Bloomington, MN 55437
888-248-0822; 800-537-2237 (MN only)
www.pacer.org
　　(The Center's Transition Parent Briefs cover such topics as preparing your child for the age of majority, person-centered planning, government benefits, preparing for employment.)

Person-Centered Planning Education Site
Cornell University
ILR School
Employment and Disability Institute
www.ilr.cornell.edu/edi/pcp/course01.html

Technical Assistance on Transition and the Rehabilitation Act
www.pacer.org/tatra

Youthhood.org
www.youthhood.org
　　(Website for young adults with disabilities to use in exploring transition issues.)

Postsecondary Education

The ACT Test
Services for Students with Disabilities
www.act.org/aap/disab/index.html

Autism-related Scholarships
www.collegescholarships.org/health/autistic-students.htm

College Board Tests
Services for Students with Disabilities
www.collegeboard.com/ssd/student/index.html

College Resources for Students with Autism
http://autismandcollege.googlepages.com

DO-IT
Disabilities, Opportunities, Internetworking, and Technology
www.washington.edu/doit

Fairtest
The National Center for Fair and Open Testing
15 Court Square, Ste. 820
Boston, MA 02108
www.fairtest.org
(Maintains a list of colleges and universities that don't require ACT/SAT for admission.)

Going to College
www.going-to-college.org
(Website for college-bound students with disabilities with online videos that teach about exploring interests, requesting accommodations, choosing a college, what to expect in college, etc.)

Health Resource Center
Online Clearinghouse on Postsecondary Education for Individuals with Disabilities
www.gwu.edu

LDonline
www.ldonline.org
(Although not specifically for students with ASD, the site has many articles on college and college preparation for students with mild learning challenges.)

National Center on Educational Outcomes
University of Minnesota
207 Pattee Hall
Minneapolis, MN 55455
612-626-1530
http://cehd.umn.edu/NCEO
(Information on accommodations, alternate assessments, graduation requirements, including links to individual state policies)

Think College
www.thinkcollege.net
(Online database of schools that offer postsecondary education for students with intellectual disabilities.)

Transition Coalition
www.transitioncoalition.org
(The website has a searchable database of 18-21 programs—community-based transition programs in age-appropriate settings for students with disabilities aged 18-21.)

Legal & Financial Issues

ADA Document Portal
National Network of ADA Centers
www.adata.org/adaportal

Building the Legacy: IDEA 2004
http://idea.ed.gov
(The U.S. Dept. of Education, Office of Special Education's official IDEA website.)

DisabilityInfo.gov
www.disabilityinfo.gov
(Includes links to information about the ADA, work incentives, government benefits such as SSI, etc.)

Footsteps for the Future
The Arc of East Middlesex
www.theemarc.org
(A form to use to create a Letter of Intent is available online by clicking on "Resources.")

GovBenefits.gov
www.govbenefits.gov

Social Security Online
www.ssa.gov

WrightsLaw
www.wrightslaw.com
(Good source of information on IDEA, NCLB, and Section 504.)

Employment

DisabilityInfo.Gov
www.disabilityinfo.gov
(The home page includes a link to a great deal of information on vocational rehabilitation services, including links to each state's agencies.)

Job Accommodation Network
www.janweb.icdi.wvu.edu

National Collaborative on Workforce and Disability
www.ncwd-youth.info

Office of Disability Employment Policy
www.dol.gov/odep

Rehabilitation Research and Training Center on Workplace Supports and Job Retention
Virginia Commonwealth University
1314 W. Main St.
Richmond, VA 23284
www.worksupport.com

U.S. Dept. of Labor
Office of Disability Employment Policy
200 Constitution Ave., NW
Washington, DC 20210
800-ODEP-DOL
www.dol.gov/odep

References & Suggested Reading

Anderson, Winifred, Chitwood, Stephen, Hayden, Deirdre, and Takemoto, Cherie. *Negotiating the Special Education Maze: A Guide for Parents and Teachers.* 4th ed. Bethesda, MD: Woodbine House, 2008.

Asperger Syndrome: Transition to College and Work. (DVD). Winston-Salem, NC: Coulter Video (www.coultervideo.com).

Attwood, Tony. *Exploring Feelings: Cognitive Behavioral Therapy to Manage Anxiety.* Arlington, TX: Future Horizons, 2004.

Baker, Jed. *Preparing for Life: The Complete Guide to Transitioning to Adulthood for Those with Autism and Asperger's Syndrome.* Arlington, TX: Future Horizons, 2006.

Bateman, Barbara. "Legal Requirements for Transition Components of the IEP." 2006. www.wrightslaw.com/info/trans.legal.bateman.htm

Brolin, Donn E. *Life-Centered Career Education: A Competency Based Approach.* Reston, VA: Council for Exceptional Children, 1989.

Coburn, Karen Levin and Madge Lawrence Kreeger. *Letting Go: A Parents' Guide to the College Years.* 4th ed.. New York: HarperCollins, 2003.

Cohen, Marlene J. and Sloan, Donna L. (2007). *Visual Supports for People with Autism: A Guide for Parents & Professionals.* Bethesda, MD: Woodbine House.

Delmolino, Lara and Harris, Sandra. *Incentives for Change: Motivating People with Autism Spectrum Disorders to Learn and Gain Independence.* Bethesda, MD: Woodbine House, 2004.

Falvey, Mary, Forest, Marsha, Pearpoint, Jack, and Rosenberg, Richard. *All My Life's a Circle: Using the Tools: Circles, MAPS, and PATHS.* Toronto, Ontario: Inclusion Press, 1997.

Forest, M. and Lusthaus, E. (1990). Everyone belongs with MAPS action planning system. *Teaching Exceptional Children, 22,* 32-35.

Gagnon, Elisa. *Power Cards: Using Special Interests to Motivate Children and Youth with Asperger Syndrome and Autism.* Shawnee Mission, KS: Autism Asperger Publishing Co., 2001.

Glasberg, Beth A. *Functional Behavior Assessment for People with Autism: Making Sense of Seemingly Senseless Behavior.* Bethesda, MD: Woodbine House, 2006.

Grandin, Temple. *Thinking in Pictures: And Other Reports from My Life with Autism.* New York, NY: Vintage Books, 2006.

Grandin, Temple, Duffy, Kate, and Attwood, Tony. *Developing Talents: Careers for Individuals with Asperger Syndrome and High-Functioning Autism.* Shawnee Mission, KS: Autism Asperger Publishing Co., 2004.

Grandin, Temple and Scariano, Margaret. *Emergence: Labeled Autistic.* New York: Warner Books, 1996.

Gray, Carol. *Comic Strip Conversations.* Arlington, TX: Future Horizons, 1994.

Gray, Carol. *The New Social Story Book.* Arlington, TX: Future Horizons, 2000.

Harpur, John. *Succeeding in College with Asperger Syndrome*. Philadelphia, PA: Jessica Kingsley, 2004.

Nadworny, John. *The Special Needs Planning Guide: How to Plan for Every Stage in Your Child's Life*. Baltimore, MD: Paul Brookes, 2007.

National Center on Educational Outcomes. "Special Topic Area: Accommodations for Students with Disabilities." 2008.
(http://cehd.umn.edu/nceo/TopicAreas/Accommodations/Accomtopic.htm)

Organization for Autism Research, Danya International, and Southwest Autism Research and Resource Center. *Life Journey Through Autism: A Guide for Transition to Adulthood*. Arlington, VA: Organization for Autism Research, 2006.
(Can be downloaded from: www.researchautism.org)

Palmer, Ann. *Realizing the College Dream with Autism or Asperger Syndrome*. Philadelphia, PA: Jessica Kingsley, 2006.

Pearpoint, Jack, O'Brien, John, & Forest, Marsha. *PATH: A Workbook for Planning Positive Possible Futures and Planning Alternative Tomorrows with Hope for Schools, Organizations, Businesses, and Families*. 2nd ed. Toronto, Ontario: Inclusion Press, 1993.

Philpot, Dorene J. "Guardianships for Children with Disabilities." 2002. www.dphilpotlaw.com/html/guardianships.html.

"Questions & Answers about Persons with Intellectual Disabilities in the Workplace and the Americans with Disabilities Act." www.eeoc.gov/ facts/intellectual_disabilities.html.

Sicile-Kira, Chantal. *Adolescents on the Autism Spectrum: A Parent's Guide to the Cognitive, Social, Physical, and Transition Needs of Teenagers with Autism Spectrum Disorders*. New York: The Berkley Publishing Group, 2006.

Timmons, Joe, Podmostko, Mary, Bremer, Christine, Lavin, Don, and Wills, Joan. *Career Planning Begins with Assessment: A Guide for Professionals Serving Youth with Educational and Career Development*

Challenges. Rev. ed. Washington, DC: National Collaborative on Workforce & Disability for Youth Institute for Educational Leadership, 2005. (Available online at: www.ncwd- youth.info under Resources & Publications, Manuals & Guides.)

United States Department of Education. "Alternate Achievement Standards for Students with the Most Significant Cognitive Disabilities: Non-regulatory Guidance." Washington, DC: U.S. DOE, 2005.

U. S. Department of Education, Office for Civil Rights. "Students with Disabilities Preparing for Postsecondary Education: Know Your Rights and Responsibilities." Washington, DC: U.S. DOE, 2007. (Available from www.ed.gov/print/about/offices/list/ocr/transition.html.)

Wright, Peter W.D. and Wright, Pamela D. *Wrightslaw: Special Education Law.* 2nd ed. Hartfield, VA: Harbor House Law Press, 2007.

Index

About the Author

Carolyn T. Bruey, Psy.D, BCBA, has been working with children with autism and their families for the past thirty years. She has published various books and chapters concerning the effective support of children and adults with autism spectrum disorders and has worked with them in both the private and public sectors.

Mary Beth Urban, M.Ed., is a special education teacher and special education consultant for secondary programs. Her twenty-one years of experience have included a variety of responsibilities related to developing transition services for students with autism and other developmental disabilities.